The Time Machine Project

A Story about Leading and Managing a Project

Phill C. Akinwale, PMP, OPM3, CAPM

Praizion media

Real world project management training solutions

Project Management Basics published by Praizion Media
P.O Box 22241, Mesa, AZ 85277
E-mail: info@praizion.com
www.praizion.com

Contributing authors:

Phill C. Akinwale, PMP, PMI-SP, PMI-RMP, OPM3, CAPM

ISBN 978-1-934579-59-9
V1
PMI®, PMBOK® and PMP® are trademarks and certification mark of the Project Management Institute which are registered in the United States and other nations.

Printed in the United States of America

Table of Contents

List of Figures

List of Tables

List of Forms

PREAMBLE

This story is based on the standard for project management published by the Project Management Institute. "*A Guide to the Project Management Body of Knowledge PMBOK® Guide.*"

I remember much earlier before I became a project manager, thinking about what life as a project manager would be. I wondered what on earth the project manager did on a daily, weekly and monthly basis. I thought one needed to be a technical expert of some sort, to be able to manage a project. How wrong I was!

As I began a journey through the world of project management, I began to realize what a project is in both academic and non-academic terms. I also learned more about the role of the project manager. I discovered that many project managers have great coordinating and management skills but little or no technical skills were required. What kept the project on track and on budget was not technical skill, it was **the ability to manage the project according to a set of rules, processes, procedures, guidelines, common sense, gut instincts and a SCHEDULE.**

Anyone with a deep understanding of certain key concepts and principles with hands-on experience should be able to manage a project effectively to "some degree" but the best project managers are not merely born or made, they transition into greatness in their roles through a combination of experience, education and the **school of hard knocks**.

After working with various project managers in more than 12 organizations, I began to see what really makes a good project manager and what makes GREAT project management.

As we journey through this book and the associated DVD, we will be studying what project management is, how project management can be used to better manage your projects and also the main purpose of project management in any organization. We will also be exploring basic definitions in project management and some scenarios of practical applications of project management.

Here Are some Key definitions that will help you as you watch the DVD Lessons and study the book:

Project

A project is a temporary endeavor undertaken to create a unique product, service or result.

Project Management

Project Management in layman's terms is managing resources (human, equipment and material) to accomplish an endeavor or create a deliverable.

Project Management Process Groups (Discussed on the DVD)

Project management can be further broken down into five groups of processes.

These groups are:

Initiating

Initiating a project means the project is being authorized by a project sponsor or initiator. It also means that the project is being commissioned and entrusted into the able hands of a project manager who is also identified through the issuance of a document called a project charter. The sponsor or senior management in few words are saying "Ms. PM, this seals the deal. Initiating also involves identifying your stakeholders. Be they the customer, sponsor or end user, you go through the process of identifying who will be affected by the project and who could affect the project.

Planning

The second group of processes is planning. The end goal of planning is developing a project management plan (a plan for how the different areas of the project will be managed on the project). Initiating outputs a project charter and a list of your stakeholders. Planning outputs a project management plan.

Executing

Thirdly, we need to execute the plan. We initiate, plan and then we execute! We put the plan into action. Executing involves the project manager keeping a close watch on the plan, ensuring that it is implemented in reality exactly as planned.

Monitoring and Controlling

The fourth group of processes is used to monitor and control the project. To monitor and control the project effectively, the project manger needs to be on top of the work results. In this group of processes, the team prevents process failure or corrects defects. This is also where deliverables are formally approved by the customer.

Closing

Finally we close the project. This is called closing. In closing the project, the team transitions the deliverable to the customer. The customer by this time has already has approved the deliverable. In this process group, the project manager closes out all the necessary administrative paper work to document the project's completion.

Project Management Knowledge Areas (Discussed on the DVD)

Project management processes can also be categorized by areas of knowledge.

The 10 Knowledge Areas are:

1. Project Integration Management – deals with effective project coordination
2. Project Scope Management – defining the project scope
3. Project Time Management – creating and managing the project schedule
4. Project Cost Management –defining and managing the budget
5. Project Quality Management –defining and managing quality
6. Project Human Resource Management –managing the team
7. Project Communications Management – defining and managing communications
8. Project Risk Management – defining and managing risks

9. *Project Procurement Management – managing contracts and agreements*

10. *Project Stakeholder Management – managing stakeholders*

These ten Knowledge Areas can be viewed as areas of knowledge critical for effective project management. Though the Project Manager need not be a certified expert in all of these areas, essential knowledge and proficiency is advised to enable effective management of all aspects of a project.

Project Management Knowledge Areas Mnemonic

I	Project Integration Management
S	Project Scope Management
TOTAL	Project Time Management
COST	Project Cost Management
QUITE	Project Quality Management
HIGH	Project Human Resource Management
CHECK	Project Communications Management
REAL	Project Risk Management
PRICE	Project Procurement Management
STATUS	Project Stakeholder Management

IS Total Cost Quite High? Check Real Price Status

	PROJECT MANAGEMENT PROCESS GROUPS				
	Initiating	Planning	Executing	Monitoring & Controlling	Closing
Project Integration Management	Develop Project Charter	Develop Project Management Plan	Direct and Manage Project Work	Monitor and Control Project Work Perform Integrated Change Control	Close Project or Phase
Project Scope Management		Plan Scope Management Collect Requirements Define Scope Create WBS		Validate Scope Control Scope	
Project Time Management		Plan Schedule Management Define Activities Sequence Activities Estimate Activity Resources Estimate Activity Durations Develop Schedule		Control Schedule	
Project Cost Management		Plan Cost Management Estimate Costs Determine Budget		Control Costs	
Project Quality Management		Plan Quality Management	Perform Quality Assurance	Control Quality	
Project Human Resource Management		Plan Human Resource Management	Acquire Project Team Develop Project Team Manage Project Team		
Project Communications Management		Plan Communications Management	Manage Communications	Control Communications	
Project Risk Management		Plan Risk Management Identify Risks Perform Qualitative Risk Analysis Perform Quantitative Risk Analysis Plan Risk Responses		Control Risks	
Project Procurement Management		Plan Procurement Management	Conduct Procurements	Control Procurements	Close Procurements
Project Stakeholder Management	Identify Stakeholders	Plan Stakeholder Management	Manage Stakeholder Engagement	Control Stakeholder Engagement	

(Left margin label, rotated: KNOWLEDGE AREAS)

Table 1: Project Management Processes and Knowledge Area Mapping

Table 3-1, Page 61 *PMBOK® Guide* Fifth Edition

Introduction

The Story So Far

Professor Zakari (born on 29 Feb 2016) is an American theoretical physicist known all over the world for his contribution at the field of quantum theory and particle physics. He has been very introspective of late, looking back at his life's achievements over the past decade when he achieved various endeavors and received several awards for his breakthroughs in Physics.

His awards include:
- Einstein Prize (APS)
- Albert Einstein World Award of Science
- Faraday Medal and Prize
- First Step to Nobel Prize in Physics
- Fluid Dynamics Prize (APS)
- Foresight Institute Feynman Prize
- Rayleigh Medal
- Richtmyer Memorial Award
- Robert A. Millikan Award
- Rutherford Medal and Prize

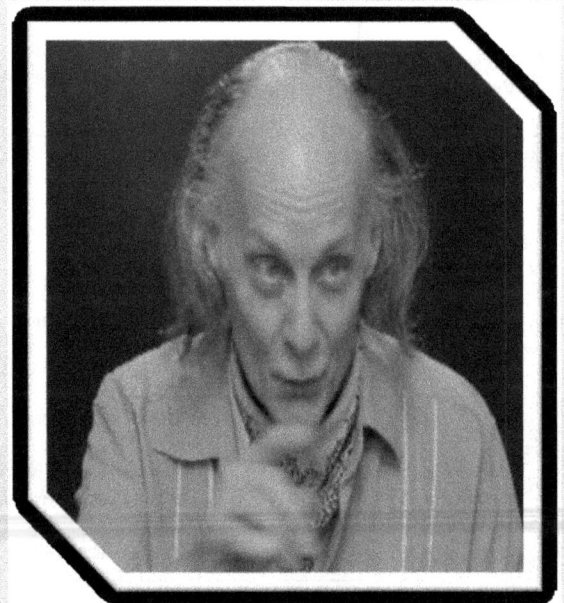

After achieving the Rutherford Medal, he embarked on a space vacation. This was the very first of its kind for an earthling. He had a vacation, resting for 2 earth years at Venus almost 25.5 million miles away from Earth. His Venus vacation spurred some extraordinary thoughts into action and now he has another great idea in mind to implement.

The world population at 2070 is now around 10 billion. It was only 5 billion when he was a little boy. Lack of space, food has significantly increased crimes all over the world and now handling crime is a top priority for all the governments of first world countries.

Consequently, Zakari wants to work more with Albert Einstein's theory of special relativity, build a time travel machine and solve the crime handling problem either by deporting offenders back in time or forwarded in future. Time travel would also prevent unknown unknown disasters by sending scouts into the future to gather future lessons learned before disasters occur. This would minimize disasters.

The Story So Far (Continued)

Professor Zakari is in discussions with various Government and Quasi-Government defense, space and time travel agencies regarding sponsoring a $55 Billion Dollars project named "TMX 01" that would last for around 15 years. At the focal point of these discussions is Noveau Inconnu, an industrial science firm and revered juggernaut in the industry. Two of its officers Alfred Pinkus (CEO) and Jonny Roberts are finalizing the possibility of Noveau Inconnu being the prime contractor.

As this happens, it has become very evident that there too many issues to consider and many times it has become so heated that various parties get mad and storm out of the meetings. Finally after six years of analysis and study, all concerned parties have come to a decision point to build a futuristic time machine that could create significant changes to the present world.

Prelude

The good news? Zakari's project is becoming a reality. This is not so good news for a particular project manager (Mary Johnson) who is being sucked into the prospective project's overwhelming details and go-no go meetings.

Mary is a project manager at the firm Noveau Inconnu who may likely be selected to drive the project to completion!

Meet the PM	
Name:	Mary Johnson
Organization:	Noveau Inconnu
Role:	Project Manager
Photo:	

PRAIZION MEDIA

Have you ever been given a seemingly unrealistic project to work on? If you have, you can relate to Mary's plight. This project is the perfect blend for a tough project:

- Unrealistic deadlines

- Tough schedule

- Contractually required WBS

- And a tough team to manage

- Mary in this first chapter gives us some insight into how this whole "nightmare" began.

Team Member Discussion

1. What is the most difficult project you have ever worked on and why?

2. Could anything have been done to make it less difficult? If so, what could have been done?

Chapter 1: Undated Diary Entry

The moment the scope of work and purchase orders for the new project at our firm hit my desk, I had a distinct feeling we would need a little more than our 530 combined years of project management experience to see us through this one.

After spending an hour scanning the project documents, I quickly realized that its stringent project performance and reporting requirements were totally different than anything I had encountered in my nine years with Noveau Inconnu. Jacks and Jills of all trades, we were, at this edgy, multidimensional firm, and we were. . .yes, we were proud of it!

Apparently, the customer, Professor Zakari, was accustomed to using highly detailed, demanding schedules to track the several projects he had worked on since Microsoft Project became such a huge hit on the PM scene. It was also clear that he had very high expectations of our firm, having come through such a rigorous bidding process. After all, our marketing staff and executive muscle boys had made certain promises (without the team's involvement), which we had to redeem.

Even our first task was a bit daunting – within sixty days, we had to draw up a humongous project schedule, detailing every single resource, right down to the hour.

Our program manager, Bill Bragg, had always touted our many years of collective experience and how that alone would see us through any project. In Bill's mind, certifications in project management and PM software had little to no value. "What is all that PMP project management certification stuff you talk about?" he was fond of saying. "You can't replace thirty years of managing projects with some so-called certificate."

Though his statement held some truth, I knew that the techniques, skills and thought processes I had learned for my qualifying project management exam, coupled with my own experience, would see me through this new project. At least I crossed my fingers and hoped I was right.

Let me tell you the story of how this "nightmare" unfolded into a futuristic dream of sorts.

SECTION 1

PROJECT SELECTION MEETING

The dreaded email...announcing you have been sucked into another meeting with Cold Pinkus, that person in the office always spreading the flu. At Noveau Inconnu, this is called...The Project selection meeting!

Here, you will observe the team reviewing various potential projects and commenting on their relevance and viability. Be it an internal capital project or a customer project, there is some form of selection or a decision point to pursue the endeavor or not.

Some companies use simple common sense to decide whether to pursue an endeavor or not, others use methods such as the methods mentioned here which include: NPV, IRR, Payback Period, BCR. See the PM101 section for more about these methods.

This is the FIRST STEP of the journey to project management. The Executive Team or Project Selection Board selects the project(s) to undertake. Not all projects will make it past this stage.

Chapter 2: Project Selection Day

Alfred Pinkus strolled into the conference room, attempting to shake hands with those unfortunate team members who hadn't scurried to the back of the conference room quickly enough. He wore an outdated suit with an alarmingly bright orange polka dot tie. He cleared his throat to capture the team's attention and began his "speech."

"Welcome to the July 2072 PSM for Noveau Inconnu. Today, we have some rather interesting potential projects. But of course you know that not every project that makes it to the PSM makes it out of the door alive."

Bill squirmed in his seat. He was still considered a "newbie" and had yet to earn the team's total respect.

"On the murder board today," Pinkus continued, "we have Jonny Roberts, Billy Bragg, Dottie Doodle, Martha Mona and Mary Johnson presiding over affairs," he said, nodding to each as he spoke. "The thing about our PSMs is,"

"What's a PMS?" Bill abruptly interrupted.

"Do you mean PSM, Billy?" quipped Pinkus with a smirk. "It appears you were not properly schooled in orientation when you came on board."

Bill turned as red as a beet. "It stands for 'Project Selection Meeting,' Billy, and this is where we review the best projects and make a selection. Remember?" asked Mary.

"Oh, yeah thanks. I get it," said Billy, still red-faced.

Pinkus shook his head. "So...as I was saying before that rather unnecessary interruption, today we will select which projects to take on. Being the industrial juggernauts that we are, we can work on absolutely anything. However, we must review some key information before moving a single step further. Here is a list of our potential projects," he said, signaling to his assistant, Liz, to activate the Holo-projector.

Everyone looked at the brightly colored images as Pinkus recited the words.

"Project 1: Build a quarter-mile bridge in Wyoming.

"Project 2: Software refresh project for the city.

"Project 3: Build a time machine for Professor Zakari, the well-renowned multibillionaire whose project our vendors flunked a decade ago. . ."

Mary waved her hand in the air in obvious disagreement. "That was our fault, Mr. Pinkus," she said. "Let's be honest here," she continued. "Those were in the early days when I had just come on board. We had no schedule, no defined budget, poor tracking mechanisms and I was the only PMP," she said.

"Oh, I see!" said Pinkus sarcastically. "Now, if I may continue," he said, motioning to the screen and rolling his eyes.

"Project 4: An inventory check for the Bijoux Corporation and an implementation of a new JIT system."

Clearing his throat, Pinkus paused for a moment and then continued. "This is not the time or place to decide who was 'right' about what happened eons ago. The question at hand is, which project should we select today? Again, let's go over our options. Project 1, the Bridge Project — NPV is $350 million. Project 2, Software refresh project - IRR is 70%. Project 3, Time Machine — payback period is fifteen years. Project 4. . ."

Bill's eyes suddenly popped wide open. "WHAT?" he exclaimed. "Who's going to wait fifteen years to get paid?"

Pinkus let out a soft sigh of frustration. "Let's read the final one, if we may," he said somewhat gruffly. "Project 4, JIT. Its BCR is four to one. Now, which project should we select?"

"Well, I think it's a no-brainer with the information we have," Mary offered.

"But the information we have is limited!" Jonny interjected. "Do we have the Net Present Values for all the projects?" he inquired. "Forget about the IRR and payback periods. All we need is the NPV to decide on this."

"Well, that's all I got from accounting. Martha?" said Pinkus, turning to the VP of HR and Finance.

"Actually, the detail is on page nine of this document," said Martha, flipping the pages. "Here it is. Please advance to page nine," she said as she proceeded to read the information aloud. "Project 1, Bridge Project, NPV is $350 million. Project 2, Software refresh project, NPV is $20 million. Project 3, Time Machine, NPV is $75 Billion."

A series of gasps echoed across the room. Martha looked up briefly and continued. "Project 4, JIT Project, NPV is $100,000."

"Well, Mr. Pinkus, I guess you see it's a no-brainer now. Except you have a valid reason not to go with Project 3. It is by far the most profitable project," said Jonny, his eyes gleaming as though he had just won the lottery.

"Well, I'm not so certain about that," Pinkus replied. "We need to be absolutely sure we can do this — as sure as can be."

"Well. . ." said Mary, standing up and pointing to her head, "think about how good it would be if we could be the first to invent a functioning time machine! Besides, we have a time machine research authority in-house."

"Exactly!" Jonny remarked. "Besides, what in this world comes without some element of risk? "

Pinkus stroked his wiry facial hair and fiddled with his glasses. "I was thinking of the software refresh project, but apparently no one else seems to be. . .what does everyone else think we should do?" he asked.

"Time machine" everyone chorused in unison.

"Well. I certainly am outnumbered. The team has spoken. Time machine it will be. I will finalize this with the board *and issue the charter for this project, and we shall all reconvene in a few days."*

Discussion

1. Does your company have a project selection process?

2. If so, describe it in a few words.

3. If not, what do you think the major topics or format of such a meeting should be?

4. How do you think bias could be reduced or eliminated from such a process?

5. What do you think the key benefits of a formal project selection process are?

SECTION 2

CREATING A PROJECT CHARTER

Developing a project charter should be a rather straightforward endeavor for the project sponsor (Jonny Roberts) but not in this case....we have a more senior overzealous stakeholder; Cold Pinkus, (the CEO) who has HIJACKED the development of the project charter! Poor Johnny!

On this project, there really should be one project sponsor! But because of the high-profile nature of this project, there is a case of the proverbial meddling CEO or Senior Executive. Pinkus the CEO has been sitting on the development of the project charter for way too long. So long that Johnny Roberts the REAL sponsor becomes frustrated and makes a call to check on Mr. Pinkus the CEO and tries to track him down. Take a look at the project charter at the end of this chapter to see the project charter Pinkus eventually finalized with Mary's help.

Chapter 3: The Project Charter
May 16th 2073

Mary returned to consciousness with a typical Pinkus summon over the intercom. When she arrived, he stood, clasped his hands together, and said, "Mary, I would like you to assist me in putting together a project charter for project TMX.01."

Mary took a seat in front of his desk as he continued. "I have a contract, business case, statement of work, and some assets from our organization's database. We must factor in how environmental factors affect the issuance of the charter and the authorization of the project. We have government approval to embark on this challenging project." And with that, he let out an unexpected belch apparently induced from his near-empty spaghetti bowl that lay nearby.

"Excuse me," he said, unashamed.

"Sure," said Mary, trying to hide her disgust. "Is this charter more like a basic document we have to create just for the sake of creating it? Or will you allow the project manager to truly take control of the project, Mr. Pinkus?" she asked.

Pinkus licked his fork and took a gulp of mineral water. "No. It is a really serious matter," Pinkus said. "This document should be referenced when identifying stakeholders, collecting requirements, defining scope and developing the project management plan. I am really a PMO convert now. I see value in the PMO," he said emphatically.

"Really?" asked Mary.

"Absolutely," he replied, taking another gulp of mineral water.

"So, in other words, the project charter will be used in certain other project management processes?" Mary confirmed.

"Precisely!" he said excitedly. "In fact, let me tell you a bit about what I learned from the Project Management for C-Level Executives class from Praizion Media last week. . . ." He opened a worn-out binder and licked his fingers as he flipped through the pages.

"Ewww, gross!" thought Mary.

Pinkus cleared his throat and proceeded to read aloud, as though he were standing at a lectern. "The approved Project Charter formally authorizes the project or a phase in the project. It is important to note that the Project Charter contains a lot of advanced information about the project, such as initial stakeholder requirements, high-level risks, a summary milestone schedule, a summary budget, measurable project objectives and related success criteria. It also establishes partnership between performing and requesting organizations. It also identifies project success factors and identifies the key decision maker to decide on the project's success and completion, and who also signs off on the project."

It must have taken only a minute, but his little "speech" felt like an hour to his hostage audience of one.

Pinkus ruffled his pile of papers and stared at Mary over the rim of his glasses. "You probably guessed that you are one of our choices for project manager since you have a star-studded list of projects under your belt, Mary. We are counting on someone as good as you to make this work."

1.   Develop Project Charter

The Develop Project Charter process is the first process in the PMBOK® Guide. The Project Charter is developed while initiating the project prior to planning.

Inputs	Tools and Techniques	Outputs
▫ Project statement of work ▫ Business case ▫ Agreements ▫ Enterprise environmental factors ▫ Organizational process assets	▫ Expert judgment ▫ Facilitation Techniques	▫ Project charter

Figure 1: Develop Project Charter: Inputs, Tools & Techniques and Outputs

Project Charter

A Project Charter is a document which:

- Is issued or created by the project initiator or sponsor who is external to the project and funds the project (Note: The project sponsor may delegate the task of creating the Project Charter to the Project Manager).

- Formally authorizes a project or phase. Approval and authorization for the project or phase is shown by the project sponsor's signature on the Project Charter (Note: The Project Charter is developed before project planning activities begin).

- Provides the Project Manager with authority to apply resources to the project (Note: It is important for the Project Manager to be assigned during the development of the Project Charter so that the Project Manager can participate in this process).

- Contains high-level information about the project such as initial stakeholder requirements, high-level risks, summary milestone schedule, summary budget, measurable project objectives and related success criteria.

  Observe the information in the project charter developed by Alfred Pinkus with Mary's assistance.

Project Charter

Project Title:	TMX 01

Project Sponsor:	Alfred Pinkus and Jonny	**Date Prepared:**	May 16, 2073
Project Manager:	Mary Johnson	**Project Customer:**	Professor Zakari

Project Purpose or Business case

The project's purpose is to plan, organize, coordinate and execute the TMX 01 project. This will research and implement a time travel machine system in order to solve the criminal handling problem by transporting back in time or into the future. The project is sponsored by a collection of quasi-government agencies. Alfred Pinkus and Jonny Roberts are the sponsors. Upon successful completion, Professor Zakari desires to sell the idea to the government so it can help track down criminals.

Project Description

Since Noveau Inconnu has extensive experience and financial reserves for high tech & expensive machines, Professor Zakari is has decided to procure services from them. Furthermore, they have had success together on teaming agreements in the last 20 years. Hence, both parties agree as follows:

- Coordination & implementation of TMX 01 project by Noveau Inconnu as defined by Professor Zakari, Alfred Pinkus and Jonny Roberts.
- In the event of any unforseen circumstances, Noveau Inconnu will do explore all possible as mentioned in the to-be finalized scope baseline.
-In case of cancellation, all payments made to date will be non-refundable and all outstanding payments will be due from the date of cancellation and can be transferred through insurance upon management decision.
-The charter may be modified if an amendment is made in writing and is signed by both parties. The failure of either party to enforce any provision shall not be a limitation of that party's right to subsequently enforce and compel strict compliance with every provision of this agreement. This agreement shall be governed by the laws of the USA.

Project and Product Requirements

The project will meet requirement after time travel machine as well as solve the criminal handling problem either by deported back in time or forwarded in future. It's fundamental requirement includes:

-Research of Albert Einstein's theory of special relativity, Mac John classic theory of relative motion
-Huge disk space depends on the initial amount of data that needs to be backed up and how much data changes on an hourly basis
-A extra high speed switching capable machine compatible with the velocity of light
-Measurements of various quantities that are relative to the velocities of observers
-Design that is compatible at high velocity when relativistic energy and momentum increases
-JenXc Programing of the machine
-Whirlpool Affinity Test, Eddies Reverse Reflux Loop Test, Black hole impact analysis
-Phase End Review

Project Acceptance Criteria

The success of the project will be determined by below mentioned criteria

-Initial plan reviews with all plans agreed by stakeholders involved (see Stakeholder Register).
-Expected result delivered to the end user/customer.
-Project implementation within desired budget, time frame and quality as per time, cost and quality management plan to be established later.
- Monitoring and controlling will be done as per agreed communication management plan.

Project Charter

Project Charter

Initial and high level Risks

* Project cancellation without any outcome: Impact: high, Probability: Medium

*data loss by virtue of no backup: Impact: high, Probability: medium

*side-effect of cloning: Impact: high, Probability: medium

*Natural influence: Impact: high, Probability: low

*Budget limit exceed due to variation of other constraint: Impact: high, Probability: high

*Schedule does not meet the deadline: Impact: medium, Probability: low

Project Objectives	Success Criteria	Person Approving
Scope		
Scope includes all the works and only the works required to transport man wholly and bodily through time. There will be two modules i.e. Forward time travel and Backward time travel modules that will provide the option to transport back in time or forward in future.	Meeting mentioned scope	Sponsor & Customer
Time		
Time duration for the project is 15 years, from 7 June 2071.	Meeting mentioned deadline	Sponsor
Cost		
The initial Budget for the project is $55 Billion Dollars.	Meeting mentioned budget	Sponsor
Quality		
The machine must meet the quality standard from ISTTO and environmental standard from IETO.	Meeting the mentioned quality standard	Sponsor
Other		
Security of the research, design, programming will be maintained strictly as mentioned in security guideline	Meeting the mentioned service	Sponsor & Customer

Key Stakeholders

Name	Role	Responsibility
Alfred Pinkus and Jonny Roberts	Sponsor	Financial support
Professor Zakari	Customer	Supporter
Noveau Inconnu	Organizer	Organizational support
Mary Johnson	PM	Manage the project
Bill Brag	Program manager	Overview and support the project
Andrew	Programmer and contributor to	Programming
Henry	Safety and Tactical advisor	Supervisor and supporter of safety issues
Mike	Mid-level manager	Coordinate all electronic issues

Project Charter

Summary Milestones

Research Completed	Year 2071
Requirements finalized	Year 2073
Prototype built	Year 2075
Design completed	Year 2077
Programing done	Year 2085
Module Test successful	Year 2086
Phase End Review completed	Year 2087

Estimated Budget

Initial budget is 55 Billion Dollars with rough order of magnitude planning. This should be split approximately 5.2 Billion Dollars per year maximum.

Project Manager Authority Level

High (by definition of Noveau Standards)

Staffing Decisions

Project Manager can recruit skilled manpower for planning, implementation, monitoring and closing of the project.

Budget Management and Variance

Budget cost not to exceed 55 Billion Dollars. Budget will managed by project manager upon acceptance of project sponsor. The maximum variance of budget is +/- 10%.

Technical Decisions

Technical decisions will be taken care by both the PM, customer and sponsor with support to a mutual agreed technical representative. Andrew and Bill Brag will also provide support in technical issues.

Conflict Resolution

Any conflict can be negotiated through mutual understanding by all parties. If any unsolvable dispute arises, it will be managed first by mediation and consequently by the lawyer.

Escalation Path for Authority Limitations

Any items or issues that are not resolved by neither the PM nor the project team will be escalated to the program manager and program controller level.

Approvals

Project Manager Signature		Sponsor or Originator Signature	
Project Manager Name		Sponsor or Originator Name	
Date		Date	

Form 1: Project Charter

Discussions

1. Does your firm follow a project chartering process?

2. What is the advantage of developing a project charter?

3. What does the term "business case" mean?

PRAIZION MEDIA

SECTION 3: ANNOUNCING THE PROJECT

SECTION 3

PROJECT ANNOUNCEMENT

The project has been authorized and it is part of a larger group of initiatives called a program. This term will be discussed in the later part of this book.

In this scene, there is a meeting of sorts to announce the authorization of the project and the efforts that will ensue in planning the project and ultimately the program.

Some organizations my bypass having a formal meeting until after all the planning is done but in this case, Alfred Pinkus feels the magnitude of the project deserves what he terms as a "Mini Kick-Off Meeting" to announce the new project and the project manager Mary.

38   WWW.PRAIZION.COM

Chapter 4: Chosen against Her Will

"Congratulations! YOU are the project manager."

The meeting started earlier than usual. All team members eagerly huddled in the boardroom, in high spirits.

"Ahem," growled Pinkus, clearing his throat. "May we have some silence, please?" The team calmed down and everyone settled into their seats.

"Both parties have decided to move ahead with project TMX.01. Total project value is $75 billion. End date is 2079," said Pinkus. "Jonny Roberts is our project sponsor. Mary, you are our chosen project manager. The project has been authorized and will commence immediately. You will report to the new program manager, Billy Bragg."

"WHAT?" exclaimed Mary. "I can't believe you chose Billy as the program manager for this project!" she blurted out, blushing as she realized she had just publicly insulted Billy.

"Well, he has worked on similar sized projects in the past," said Pinkus, making eye contact with Billy.

"Give a new boy a chance. I have earned my stripes," Billy said with a grin. "Besides, the Project Charter issued by the sponsor authorizes the project and authorizes YOU to apply resources to the project," Billy continued.

"Indeed," said Pinkus, nodding. "It contains a lot of high-level information about this endeavor. There are your marching orders, Mary. Run with it!" said Pinkus very officiously. "This is all you need to make this project successful – authority and just enough high-level project information. I need you to get all the requirements, plans and schedules in shape for this endeavor."

SECTION 4

STAKEHOLDER IDENTIFICATION

In this scene, Mary Muses over the large task ahead of her and how to identify all the stakeholders involved in this massive project. She thinks about the enormous magnitude and challenges and how to do a thorough job of identifying and including all relevant entities in the discussions.

Chapter 5: Reflecting

Diary Entry

In the meeting, Pinkus announced the issuance of the project charter and addressed any concerns about the project. I have been saddled with a monstrosity! How in the world am I going to get this project to work? Especially with meddlesome Billy as a PROGRAM MANAGER! Goodness!

The project start date and likely peak times are major concerns to Jonny, who supposedly has lots of experience in similar projects, but his suggestion to buy more time was shut down by "the suits." I feel I am just a figurehead project manager. Heaven help me!

I really have to make this happen now that I have been given the authority to apply all resources to this project. I will do my very best to make TMX.01 a success.

Chapter 6: Next Steps

Diary Entry

In this next stage of the project, the fun begins. We must identify every single stakeholder! Zakari is the customer but we have several other entities to notify. These include various entities: persons, groups or organizations that may be affected by the project (positively or negatively) or have an interest in the project's long-term effects. This is a never before implemented technology! Who wouldn't want to be in the know about this? I dread the very thought of tons of

Stakeholders emerging out of the woodwork all through the project up till the 99th hour! Dan asked me "how do we proceed with this huge task?" The truth is I honestly don't know! I will be seeking expert judgment from a variety of sources: people who have worked on other R&D projects. I will start off by studying the charter and asking Pinkus and some of our board members, for pointers. This is not one of my strengths!

SECTION 4

STAKEHOLDER MANAGEMENT CONCERNS

Mary is still having sleepless nights about her project. This is typical. If you have ever worked on a project that you are almost clueless about, it will make perfect sense. The key thing to remember though is that the PM is not the SME. The PM should include and involve all parties that could move the project closer to its goal, so when you feel overwhelmed about you project, harness the power of your learned colleagues and those who could lend you some expert judgment and give you a balanced perspective. For effective stakeholder engagement a few rules are:

BE A PROBLEM SOLVER - "Anyone not ready for problems when working with stakeholders is not ready to win."

POSITION YOURSELF FOR BUY IN - Stakeholders first buy into leadership potential of the PM before buying into project success potential

INTENTIONALLY PLAN FOR STAKEHOLDERS - Successful project managers plan ahead for their stakeholders and that pays off in the long run

DISENGAGED STAKEHOLDERS ARE YOUR RESPONSIBILITY - Stakeholder engagement depends on solid stakeholder strategy execution! There is no such thing as a disengaged stakeholder only an incapable project manager

COMMUNICATE TO COLLABORATE - Communication fuels Collaboration.

COLLABORATE TO CELEBRATE - Collaboration fuels Celebration

Remember to take a look at your templates for Stakeholder Management and see the stakeholder register that Mary came up with.

Chapter 7: Concerned
Diary Entry

I have been very concerned about involving everyone who needs to be involved on this project. I mean, with all the agencies, such as defense and space, this project has grown a hundred arms and legs in just a few months! The main customer is just ONE of my stakeholders. Now I am being told that this is just the beginning! Imagine that!

2. Identify Stakeholders

The Identify Stakeholders process involves identifying stakeholders and capturing stakeholder information in a Stakeholder Register. Prior to planning the project, the Stakeholder Register is developed during the initiating process group. The Project Manager is responsible for identifying and managing stakeholders throughout the project. The Identify Stakeholders process involves identifying entities: persons, groups or organizations who may be affected by the project (positively or negatively) or those who have an interest in the long term effects of the project.

Inputs	Tools and Techniques	Outputs
▪ Project charter ▪ Procurement documents ▪ Enterprise environmental factors ▪ Organizational process assets	▪ Stakeholder analysis ▪ Expert judgment ▪ Meetings	▪ Stakeholder register

Figure 2: Identify Stakholders: Inputs, Tools & Techniques and Outputs

Stakeholder Register

A Stakeholder Register is a key output from the Identify Stakeholders process. The Stakeholder Register is a list that identifies all relevant stakeholders who are to be included in project communications. It contains the following:

Identification Information: stakeholder name, organizational position, location, role and contact.

Assessment Information: requirements, expectations, potential influence and life-cycle phase of most interest.

Stakeholder Classification: internal/external/neutral/resistor.

Stakeholder Register

Project Title	TMX 01								

Project Manager		Mary Johnson				Date Prepared	February 14, 2073	Last Updated	February 16, 2073

Name	Position	Company	Contact	Role	Requirement	Expectation	Influence/ Interest	Power/ Impact	category
Alfred Pinkus and Jonny Roberts	Sponsor	Noveau Inconnu	969-4735-199	Financial support	All activity	Financial support	High	High	A
Professor Zakari	Customer	Independent	467-5105-898	Support	All activity	Supporter	High	High	A
Mary Johnson	PM	Noveau Inconnu	892-2861-312	Manage and organize the project	All activity	All the activity	High	High	A
Bill Brag	Program manager	Noveau Inconnu	638-6320-801	Overview and project support	All activity	Overview	Moderate	Moderate	C
Andrew	Team member	Noveau Inconnu	384-6655-901	Programmer and contributor to meetings	Programming phase	Programming support	Moderate	High	B
Henry	Team member	Noveau Inconnu	134-8593-270	Safety and Tactical advisor	All activity	Security support	Moderate	High	B
Mike	Mid-level manager	Noveau Inconnu	476-5452-495	Electronics Coordinator	Researching phase	Researcher	Moderate	High	B
Michael Mathieu	Adaptive mesh refinement	Independent	472-4226-157	Support	Researching phase	Researcher	Moderate	High	B
Max Planck	Cosmologic designer	Max pauel Designer	786-6495-225	Design support	Designing phase	Designing support	Moderate	High	B
Ney Dimaculangan	Team member	Transcom Tech Ltd	565-7164-369	Dynamic field researcher	Researching phase	Researcher	Moderate	High	B
Maria Aragon	Accounts manager	Noveau Inconnu	139-1982-131	Cost control activity	All activity	Total project support	High	High	A
Alan Turing	Team member	Noveau Inconnu	638-1939-456	Socio-cognitive Linguistics	All activity	Translation	High	High	A
Thyro Alfaro	Fluid specialist	Independent	155-4088-726	Fluid dynamics support	Researching phase	Researcher	High	High	A
Oh Jin-Hyek	Relativity tester	Independent	987-2197-387	Relativity Certified Administrator	Testing phase	Testing support	High	High	A
Tirunesh Dibaba	JenXc Programmer	Independent	670-5406-957	Programming support	Programming phase	Programming support	High	High	A
Sally Pearson	Team member	Noveau Inconnu	873-5770-859	Programming support	Programming phase	Programming support	High	High	A
Natalya Antyukh	Team member	Max pauel Designer	819-1717-420	Design support	Programming phase	Designing support	Moderate	Moderate	B

Form 1: Stakeholder Register

Stakeholder Register

Project Title		TMX 01			

Project Manager	Mary Johnson		**Date Prepared**	14-Mar-73	**Last Updated**	16-Sep-73

Power/ Interest Grid of Stakeholders

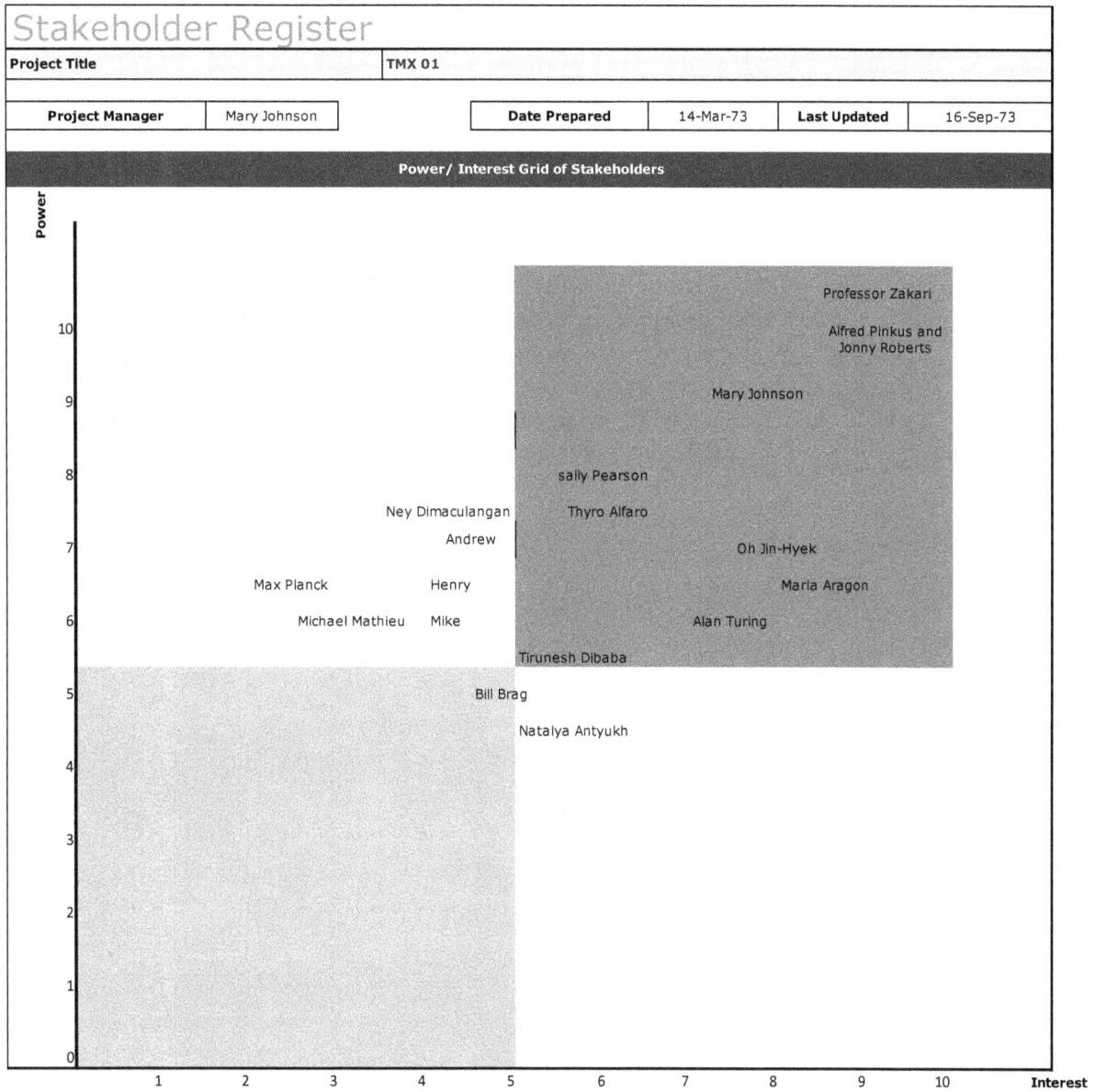

Form 2: Stakeholder Analysis

Group Discussion

- Why is it important to have a Project Charter?
- Discuss the disadvantages of not having a Project Charter.
- Who is responsible for developing the Project Charter?
- Which is the best project selection method to use?
- What is Present Value?
- Why is it important to identify stakeholders?
- What can you do to better identify your stakeholders?
- From which process do you obtain the Stakeholder Management Strategy?
- How often do you meet with stakeholders on your current project? Why not more or less?
- Who is the most powerful stakeholder on your project and why do you think so?
- What is the best way to manage difficult and powerful stakeholders?
- What is the best way to manage powerful but easy-going stakeholders who do not perform assigned tasks on your project in a timely way?
- Are all your stakeholders satisfied with performance on your current project? If no, what can you do to rectify this?

SECTION 5

DEVELOPING A PROJECT MANAGEMENT PLAN

This next scene marks the beginning of another stage: The development of the project management plan. This is a key continuous step on any project. There is a lot of information to be captured in the planning stage. Watch the team as they weave through the different pieces of this project management plan. Terms mentioned here include the WBS, Scope Statement, Cost Baseline, Schedule, Resource lists, and more.

Remember to take a look at your templates for the Project Management Plan (which is a collection of many different subsidiary plans). See what Mary came up with.

Planning the project "in plain terms"

Projects should be thoroughly planned to ensure that when project execution begins, there will be a plan and a set of guidelines to follow. This ensures that the project stays on track. The major goal and output of Planning is called the **Project Management Plan**. Planning the project involves deciding what the scope, time and cost of the project will be in totality.

Project teams must plan how to *develop* the Project Management Plan in the first place though! Will it be a detailed or high level plan? The Project Management Plan is developed by working on different aspects of it incrementally, because the Project Management Plan is a huge plan and depends on several inputs. In other words, it contains several sub-plans (known as subsidiary plans). Several little plans make up the big Project Management Plan.

Mary's job as the Project Manager is to:

- Develop the Project Management Plan.
- Ensure that the Project Management Plan is as complete and comprehensive as can be.
- Ensure the Project Management Plan contains all needed documentation.
- Update the plan with the team throughout the project as needed.

Noveau Inconnu is building a time machine and we know so many vendors and resources are working on the project. Planning the project will give all project stakeholders a *reference or baseline* of time, cost and scope expectations to follow. This baseline gives stakeholders an idea of the total scope of the project so they understand what work is required to deliver project results. While planning the project, the Project Manager leads the team in developing a schedule. This will require the Project Manager to work with the different vendors and resources, to create a timeline for each activity and determine activity dependencies. It will also enable the Project Manager calculate how long it will take to accomplish all the work required.

This is done by carrying out certain processes and using certain tools and techniques of project management. Let's discuss some of these processes and the sub-plans or baselines they give the team.

3. Develop Project Management Plan

The Develop Project Management Plan process involves developing the Project Management Plan which documents all the actions needed to develop and manage its subsidiary plans. This process:

- Defines how to integrate and coordinate all subsidiary plans that make up the Project Management Plan.
- Defines how the project will be executed, monitored, controlled and closed.
- Produces the Project Management Plan which is, progressively elaborated and controlled via the Perform Integrated Change Control process.

Ensures that the Project Management Plan is approved by key stakeholders and management.

Inputs	Tools and Techniques	Outputs
⊙ Project charter ⊙ Outputs from other processes ⊙ Enterprise environmental factors ⊙ Organizational process assets	⊙ Expert judgment ⊙ Facilitation techniques	⊙ Project management plan

Figure 3: Develop Project Management Plan: Inputs, Tools & Techniques and Outputs

Outputs from Other Processes

These outputs are from other processes that create subsidiary plans and baselines from the processes in the Planning Process Group. It also includes incremental approved updates and changes to the project management plan from the Executing and Monitoring & Controlling Process Groups

Project Management Plan

The Project Management Plan is a collection of all the subsidiary plans of the planning Process Group. It outlines how the project will be planned, executed, monitored, controlled and closed across all Knowledge Areas. It documents all outputs of the Planning Process Group, subsidiary plans, baselines and other components.

These subsidiary plans and baselines include:

- Baselines

  - Scope Baseline

  - Cost Performance Baseline

  - Schedule Baseline

- Subsidiary plans

  - Configuration Management Plan

  - Change Management Plan

  - Scope Management Plan

  - Requirements Management Plan

  - Schedule Management Plan

  - Cost Management Plan

  - Quality Management Plan

  - Process Improvement Plan

  - Human Resource Plan

  - Communications Management Plan

  - Risk Management Plan

  - Procurement Management Plan

The Project Management Plan is progressively elaborated and as the project evolves, it is updated.

Praizion Media

Project Title: _____

Project Manager: _____

Project Management Plan Strategy

Attach All Subsidiary Plans and Baselines

DEVELOP WITH YOUR TEAM. COMPILE THE TABLE SECTIONS WITH THE BEST INFORMATION AVAILABLE

Item	Subsidiary Plans	High-Level Approach	Processes Used
1	Scope Management Plan		
2	Requirements Management Plan		
3	Schedule Management Plan		
4	Cost Management Plan		
5	Quality Management Plan		
6	Process Improvement Plan		
7	Human Resources Management Plan		
8	Communications Management Plan		
9	Risk Management Plan		
10	Procurement Management Plan		
11	Change Management Plan		
12	Configuration Management Plan		

Item	Baselines	High-Level Approach	Processes Used
13	Scope Baseline		
14	Schedule Baseline		
15	Cost Performance Baseline		

Form 3: Project Management Plan (Strategy)

4. Plan Scope Management Process

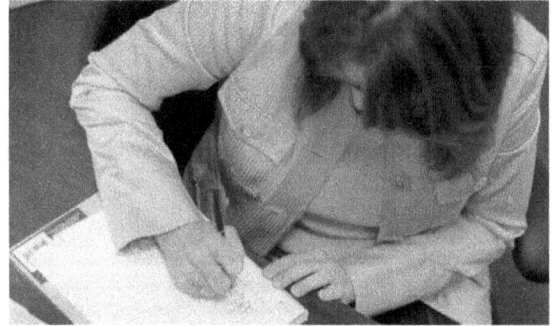

The first step in planning scope is planning how scope will be managed and how requirements will be gathered and planning how to prevent unauthorized work from being added to the project scope. This information is documented in a Scope Management Plan and a Requirements Management Plan (see examples in the pages ahead after this section).

The main goal of Plan Scope Management is developing a scope management plan, which specifies how project scope will be defined, how the end product will be validated by the customer and how scope will be controlled.

The scope management plan provides the project manager and the team with a road map for how to manage scope on the project, from start to finish. It gives guidance on how to control scope and a strategy for preventing scope creep and gold plating. The end goal of a project isn't to deliver more; it is to deliver what is required with zero tolerance for gold plating and fancy additions that were not asked for.

Inputs	Tools and Techniques	Outputs
• Project management plan • Project charter • Enterprise environmental factors • Organizational process assets	• Expert judgment • Meetings	• Scope management plan • Requirements management plan

Figure 4: Plan Scope Management: Inputs, Tools & Techniques and Outputs

Scope Management Plan

The Scope Management Plan is the roadmap for how to define scope, collect requirements and create the WBS. It defines how scope will be monitored and controlled. The Scope Management Plan is a subsidiary plan of the Project Management Plan. It defines what constitutes formal deliverable acceptance by the customer or key stakeholders. It also documents the process for managing scope changes.

Scope Management Plan

Project Title:		TMX 01		
Project Sponsor:	Alfred Pinkus and Jonny Roberts		**Date Prepared:**	28-Apr-73
Project	Mary Johnson		**Project**	Professor Zakari

Purpose

The Scope Management Plan is the roadmap for how to define scope, collect requirements and create the WBS. It defines how scope will be monitored and controlled. The Scope Management Plan is a subsidiary plan of the Project Management Plan. It defines what constitutes formal deliverable acceptance by the customer or key stakeholders. It also documents the process for managing scope changes.

Scope Management Procedure and Approaches

Mary Johnson together with the project team member and Alfred Pinkus & Jonny Roberts will ensure that scope is defined, identified, analyzed, and managed throughout the life cycle of the TMX 01 project. They will ensure scope-creep is identified as early as possible.

Defining Scope

Key and selected stakeholders will be involved to define scope and solidify the Scope Baseline. When ever any possible additional uncaptured scope is identified, it will be documented as a change-request for review of the CCB and will also be communicated in status meetings to all stakeholders.

Deliverable Acceptance

• Mary Johnson will deliver an Acceptance form to the Approver with each Deliverable or sub-deliverable. The Acceptance form will identify the deliverable and the acceptance criteria. Mary Johnson will sign the acceptance form indicating that the deliverable meets all requirements.
• Upon receipt of the Deliverable and Acceptance form, the relevant Stakeholder/Approver has 10 working days to formally approve or reject the Deliverable. The form must be marked approved or disapproved. Rejection by default is not an option. "Conditional" approvals are not permitted as they would not be handled any differently than rejection of approval.
• If the Deliverable is disapproved, a detailed description of why it was rejected must be included on the form. All errors and omissions must be detailed in the first rejection.
• If the disapproval is based on factors that were not identified in the acceptance criteria, the Approver must submit a change request to add the factors to the acceptance criteria and the Project Manager will reschedule the due dates for the deliverable based on the change request.
• E-mail approval with the approver's name typed on the form is an acceptable form of transmittal. When e-mail approvals are used, the e-mail with the approval should be saved as a text document and pasted into the acceptance form at the end of the form. Verbal approvals are not acceptable.

Project Manager Signature		Sponsor or Originator Signature	
Project Manager Name		Sponsor or Originator Name	
Date		Date	

Form 4: Scope Management Plan

Requirements Management Plan

This is a plan describing how stakeholder requirements will be captured, tracked, reported, changed and prioritized on the project from start to finish, documenting the method for executing, monitoring, controlling and closing out project requirements.

Requirements Management Plan

Project Title:		TMX 01		
Project Sponsor:	Alfred Pinkus and Jonny Roberts		Date Prepared:	28-Apr-33
Project Manager:	Mary Johnson		Project Customer:	Professor Zakari

Purpose

The plan defines how requirements associated with TMX 01 project will be identified, analyzed and documented. This is a plan describing how stakeholder requirements will be captured, tracked, reported, changed and prioritized on the project from start to finish, documenting the method for executing, monitoring, controlling and closing out project requirements.

Requirements Aspect	Approach	Responsibility	Timing/Frequency
Requirements Collection	Interviews Focus Groups Facilitated Workshops Questionnaires & Surveys Group decision-making techniques Group creativity techniques Prototypes	Mary Johnson & Team	Beginning and through Project as needed
Requirements Categorization	Requirements will be grouped as: • Business requirements • Project requirements • Product requirements • Functional requirements • Non-functional requirements (service levels, security compliance and supportability) • Quality requirements Stakeholder requirements • Acceptance criteria and business rules	Mary Johnson & Team	Beginning and through Project as needed
Requirements Prioritization	• Qualify requirements (High, Medium, Low) • Prioritization formula • VOC • Stakeholder voting process • Delphi	Mary Johnson, Prof. Zakari, Bill Bragg, Alfred Pinkus & Team.	Beginning and through Project as needed
Requirements Traceability Structure	Traceability fields: • ID Requirement • Priority • Category • Source • WBS • Display • Verification • Validation.	Mary Johnson & Team	Beginning and through Project as needed
Requirements Verification	All requirements should be verified via testing or inspection.	Mary Johnson, Prof. Zakari, Bill Bragg, Alfred Pinkus & Team	Beginning and through Project as needed
Requirements-Related Metrics	Complete, consistent, traceable, current, not-ambiguous, verifiable, ranked	Mary Johnson, Prof. Zakari, Bill Bragg, Alfred Pinkus & Team	Beginning and through Project as needed

Form 5: Requirements Management Plan

5. Collect Requirements Process

Also when planning, the team must gather ALL product and project requirements. This enables the team understand what is required for the project to be successful. These requirements are then captured in requirements documentation and a requirements traceability matrix.

Collect Requirements is the process of collecting, defining and documenting all requirements and needs from project stakeholders. The project's success hinges on the efficient documentation and management of sponsor, customer and other stakeholder expectations, needs and requirements.

Requirements could be either one of the following:

Project requirements: business requirements and project management requirements.

Product requirements: technical requirements, security requirements and performance requirements.

Inputs	Tools and Techniques	Outputs
▫ Scope management plan ▫ Requirements management plan ▫ Stakeholder management plan ▫ Project charter ▫ Stakeholder register	▫ Interviews ▫ Focus groups ▫ Facilitated workshops ▫ Group creativity techniques ▫ Group decision making techniques ▫ Questionnaires and surveys ▫ Observations ▫ Prototypes ▫ Benchmarking ▫ Context diagrams ▫ Document analysis	▫ Requirements documentation ▫ Requirements traceability matrix

Figure 5: Collect Requirements: Inputs, Tools & Techniques and Outputs

Requirements documentation

Requirements documentation describes how stakeholder requirements meet business needs.

Requirements Documentation

Project Title			TMX 01	
Project Manager	Mary Johnson	**Date Prepared** February 15, 2033	**Last Updated**	February 15, 2033

Purpose
The document establishes the framework and performance baseline for TMX 01 project.

Stakeholder Name	Requirements	Priority	Acceptance criteria
Alfred Pinkus and Jonny Roberts	Financial support for all activity	High	Meeting the cost baseline
Professor Zakari	Support for all activity	High	Maximum utilization of common resources and release resources as soon as possible
Mary Johnson	Manage and organize all activity of the project	High	Meeting all the milestone on schedule and budget
Bill Brag	Overview and support project	High	Availability of all resources on time and quantity
Andrew	Programming at programming stage and contributor to meetings	High	Successful completion of programming stage
Henry	Ensure safety and provide tactical advice at all activity	High	Successful completion of safety issue in terms of data, machine as well as overall project
Mike	Coordinate all electronics issues at research phase	High	Successful completion of research phase
Michael Mathieu	Support at research phase	Moderate	Successful completion of research phase
Max Planck	Design support	Moderate	Successful completion of design phase
Ney Dimaculangan	Dynamic field research at research phase	Moderate	Successful completion of research phase
Maria Aragon	Work on costing control at all activity	High	Successful project completion on budget
Alan Turing	Socio-cognitive Linguistics	High	Ensure communication throughout the project
Thyro Alfaro	Support on fluid dynamics at research phase	Moderate	Successful completion of research phase
Oh Jin-Hyek	Relativity Certified Administrator	High	Successful completion of research and design phase
Tirunesh Dibaba	Programming support at programming phase	Moderate	Successful completion of programming stage
Sally Pearson	Programming support at programming phase	Moderate	Successful completion of programming stage
Natalya Antyukh	Design support at design phase	Moderate	Successful completion of design phase

Form 6: Requirements Documentation

Requirements Traceability Matrix

This is a table that describes and links a requirement to its origin and traces it throughout the project life cycle.

Requirements Traceability Matrix

Project Title	TMX 01						
Project Manager	Mary Johnson	**Date Prepared**	20-Feb-72	**Last Updated**	24-Feb-76		

Purpose							
This document will link TMX 01 requirements from their origin to the deliverables that satisfy Professor Zakari's specifications.							

Information Requirement & Relationship Traceability

ID	Requirement	Priority	Category	Source	WBS Display	Verification	Validation
1	Achieve milestones on time, on budget with required quality	High	A	Professor Zakari		Sponsor	PM
2	Successful completion of project	High	A	Professor Zakari		Sponsor	PM
3	Utilization of appropriate resources	High	A	Noveau Inconnu		PM	PM
4	Management	High	A	PM		Sponsor	Program manager
5	Support	Moderate	B	Members of the project		Sponsor	PM
6	Mandatory requirement (Module- 1)	High	A	PM	2.1.1	PM	Sponsor
7	Optional requirement (Module- 1)	Moderate	B	PM	2.1.2	PM	Sponsor
8	Mandatory requirement (Module- 2)	High	A	PM	2.2.1	PM	Sponsor
9	Optional requirement (Module- 2)	Moderate	B	PM	2.2.2	PM	Sponsor
10	Conflict Resolution	Moderate	B	PM	3.2.2	PM	Program manager
11	Final prototype	High	A	PM	3.4.3	Max Planck	Program manager
12	Develop an interface	High	A	PM	4.4.1	PM	Program manager
13	Execution of programing (module-1)	High	A	PM	5.1.2	Tirunesh Dibaba	Program manager
14	Testing (module-1)	High	A	PM	5.1.3	Tirunesh Dibaba	Program manager
15	Execution of programing (module-2)	High	A	PM	5.2.2	Tirunesh Dibaba	Program manager
16	Testing (module-2)	High	A	PM	5.2.3	Tirunesh Dibaba	Program manager
17	Short out limitations(module-1)	Moderate	B	PM	7.1.2	PM	Sponsor
18	Short out limitations(module-2)	Moderate	B	PM	7.2.2	PM	Sponsor

Form 7: Requirements Traceability Matrix

6.   Define Scope

The team further defines the project in a detailed narrative and further elaborates on project scope in a Project Scope Statement.

Defining project scope is essential to the overall success of a project because it is in this process that the Project Team creates the Project Scope Statement. Existing risks, assumptions and constraints are analyzed for completeness and any necessary additions are made. The Define Scope process entails:

- Developing a detailed Project Scope Statement
- Clarifying details about project deliverables
- Analyzing existing risks, assumptions and constraints for completeness.

The Project Team documents this information in the Project Scope Statement which is the key output of this process.

Inputs	Tools and Techniques	Outputs
<ul><li>Scope management plan</li><li>Project charter</li><li>Requirements documentation</li><li>Organizational process assets</li></ul>	<ul><li>Expert judgment</li><li>Product analysis</li><li>Alternatives generation</li><li>Facilitated Workshops</li></ul>	<ul><li>Project scope statement</li><li>Project documents updates</li></ul>

Figure 6: Define Scope: Inputs, Tools & Techniques and Outputs

Project Scope Statement

A Project Scope Statement is a detailed description of the project deliverables and the work required to produce the deliverables. The Project Scope Statement also includes descriptions about project constraints, project assumptions, project exclusions, product scope and user acceptance criteria.

Project Scope Statement

Project Title:		TMX 01	

Project Sponsor:	Alfred Pinkus and Jonny Roberts	Date Prepared:	14-Feb-33
Project Manager:	Mary Johnson	Project Customer:	Professor Zakari

Product scope

The purpose of the time travel machine is to help solve the criminal handling problem either by transporting back in time or forward in future. There is a need for Mac John's classic theory of relative motion. The product will also ensure immeasurable disk space based on the initial amount of data that needs to be backed up and how much data changes on an hourly basis. The machine should have extra high speed switching capable & compatible with the velocity of light. The measurements should be established for various scenarios that are relative to the velocities of observers. Designs have to be compatible at high velocity when relativistic energy and momentum increases. The machine programming will be done on advanced JenXc whereas tests will be measured through Whirlpool Affinity Test, Eddies Reverse Reflux Loop Test and Black hole impact analysis.

Project Deliverables

The Time travel machine will meet the following main deliverables:
* One machine will handle problems by deporting offenders back in time and other one by sending offenders into the future. See design document on shared drive for details.
* The TMX01 Event Store (BLUE BOX) will be established for hidden log management that OSX keeps on each HFSX+ formatted disk/partition of changes made to the data on it.
* A relatively small system will use a giawire 909 air-fi drive that is far faster than a larger system being backed-up wirelessly to a Time Capsule.
*A TMX01-S drive will proctor how incremental backups are, in effect, full backups (TANX BX). VMAir-Links act like aliases in the system, and are the key to how the Time Machine backs up modified data, but have each backup be, in effect, a full backup of everything that was on the TMX01 at Point X. Backups Storage (GREEN and PINK BOXES) will be a single internal disk (our Startup Disk) to a single disk or Time Capsule.

Exclusions

The project will have below exclusions:
-This project will not address space deportation of offenders.
- The project is not intended to address offender particularization theories postulated by the HSG Agency
-Travel limited to 777AD - 3500AD and excludes any prior of future dates outside this bracket
-Fixed path exclusions: TX Backup should be excluded with the FUT-option whether or not the item exists.
-The scope of travel is for just 1 Traveller. Multi-passenger travel is excluded

Acceptance Criteria

The success of the project will be determined by below mentioned criteria
-Initial plan reviews and agreed by stakeholder involved.
-Expected result delivered to the end user.
-Project implementation with desired budget, time frame and quality as per time, cost and quality management plan to be established later.
- Monitoring and controlling will be done as per agreed communication management plan.

Constraints

Project must be completed to coincide with new governmental agency regulation implementation
-12 Key Scientists multi-booked on core pressing projects across 5 sister agencies
-Stochastic precedence constraints
-Approach for building TMX based on unfounded theories - absolute precision lacking

Assumptions

The people of the future would certainly be infinitely ahead of us in all their appliances. They would come without arms, medicine or anything to eat. It would be in-built in armor or bone deep. Agressors would not return as a result of large differences in handling offendors. Particulization theory likely to be in effect.

Form 8: Project Scope Statement

7. Create WBS

The WBS is a hierarchical (also often graphical) depiction of work to be done on the project. It defines the scope of the project by subdividing the work into smaller more manageable pieces. Each descending level of the WBS contains greater level of detail regarding the project work. The WBS is created by the Project Team. These lowest levels of the WBS (work packages) will be further decomposed into an activity list later on in the project.

Inputs	Tools and Techniques	Outputs
▪ Scope management plan ▪ Project charter ▪ Requirements documentation ▪ Organizational process assets	▪ Expert judgment ▪ Product analysis ▪ Alternatives generation ▪ Facilitated Workshops	▪ Project scope statement ▪ Project documents updates

Figure 7: Define Scope: Inputs, Tools & Techniques and Outputs

WBS

A Work Breakdown Structure (WBS) is used to show a hierarchical break down of project deliverables into smaller components. Each descending level of the WBS represents a detailed definition of the project deliverable. Each WBS component is connected to a control account and assigned a unique identifier called a code of accounts.

In the WBS for manufacturing a custom line of cars, at the topmost node you could have "Automobile Project". Underneath that you could have different branches: Body, Chassis and Suspension, Engine & Transmission and Interior, for example.

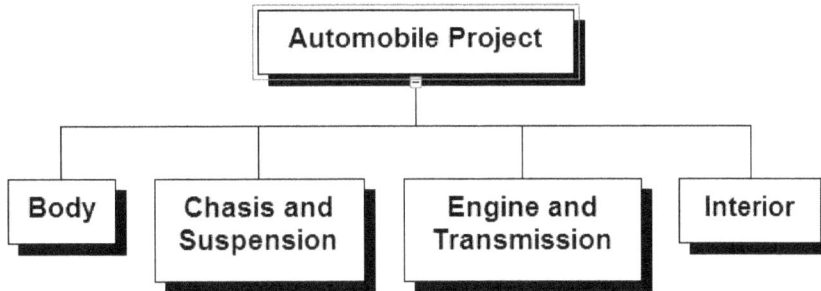

Figure 8: High-Level Automobile Project WBS Grouped by Nature of Work

Alternatively, the project could be broken down into the different custom vehicles. For example, A class, B class and C class.

The overall idea is to decompose the work so that the project scope becomes more apparent to the team and easier to manage and track. The WBS may be several levels.

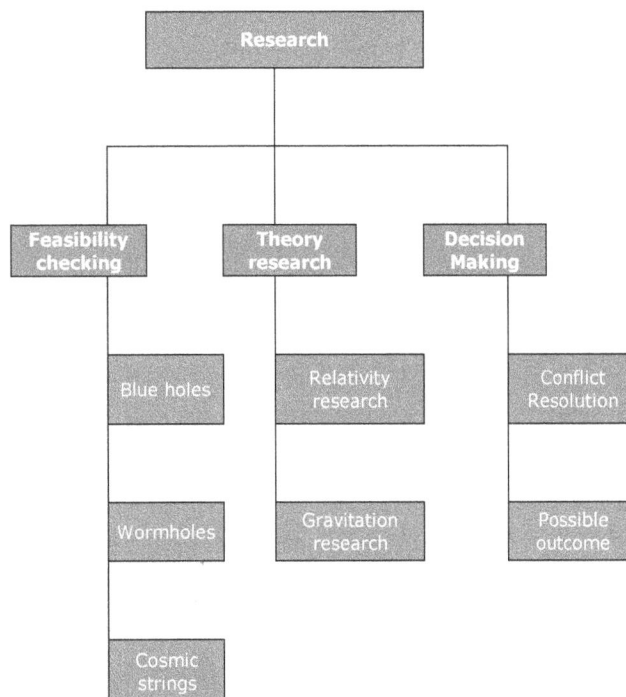

Figure 9: Cross Section of TXM01 WBS Branch

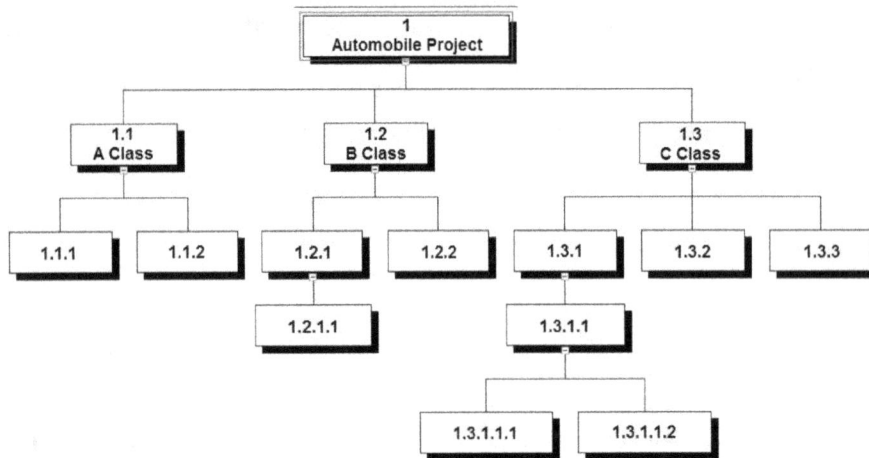

Figure 10: Example of a WBS

Work Package

A work package is the smallest component of a WBS. Work packages can be scheduled, measured, estimated, monitored and controlled. A work package is connected to a control account in the WBS. In the figure above, 1.3.1.1.1 is a work package.

Control Account

A control account is a management control point of the WBS above the work package level which helps define a framework for schedule reporting such as Earned Value reporting. Control accounts may contain one or more work packages but a work package can only be associated with one control account. In the figure above, node 1.3 (C Class) is a control account.

Code of Accounts

A code of accounts is a numbering system used as a unique identifier for each component of the WBS. The identifiers 1.1.1, 1.2.1.2, 1.3.3 etc in the figure above are unique identifiers known as code of accounts.

Planning Package

A WBS component with un-decomposed work content above the work package level but below the control account level. It can be described as a "holding-account" of work that is not at the time practicable to decompose further to the work package level. Planning packages are used to plan work to be accomplished in the future at a high-level only decomposing the work later in time as the scheduled time period for the work approaches. 1.1.1 and 1.3.3 are examples of planning packages.

Work Breakdown structure

Project Title	TMX 01

Project Manager	Mary Johnson
Date Prepared	February 17, 2072
Last Updated	February 20, 2072

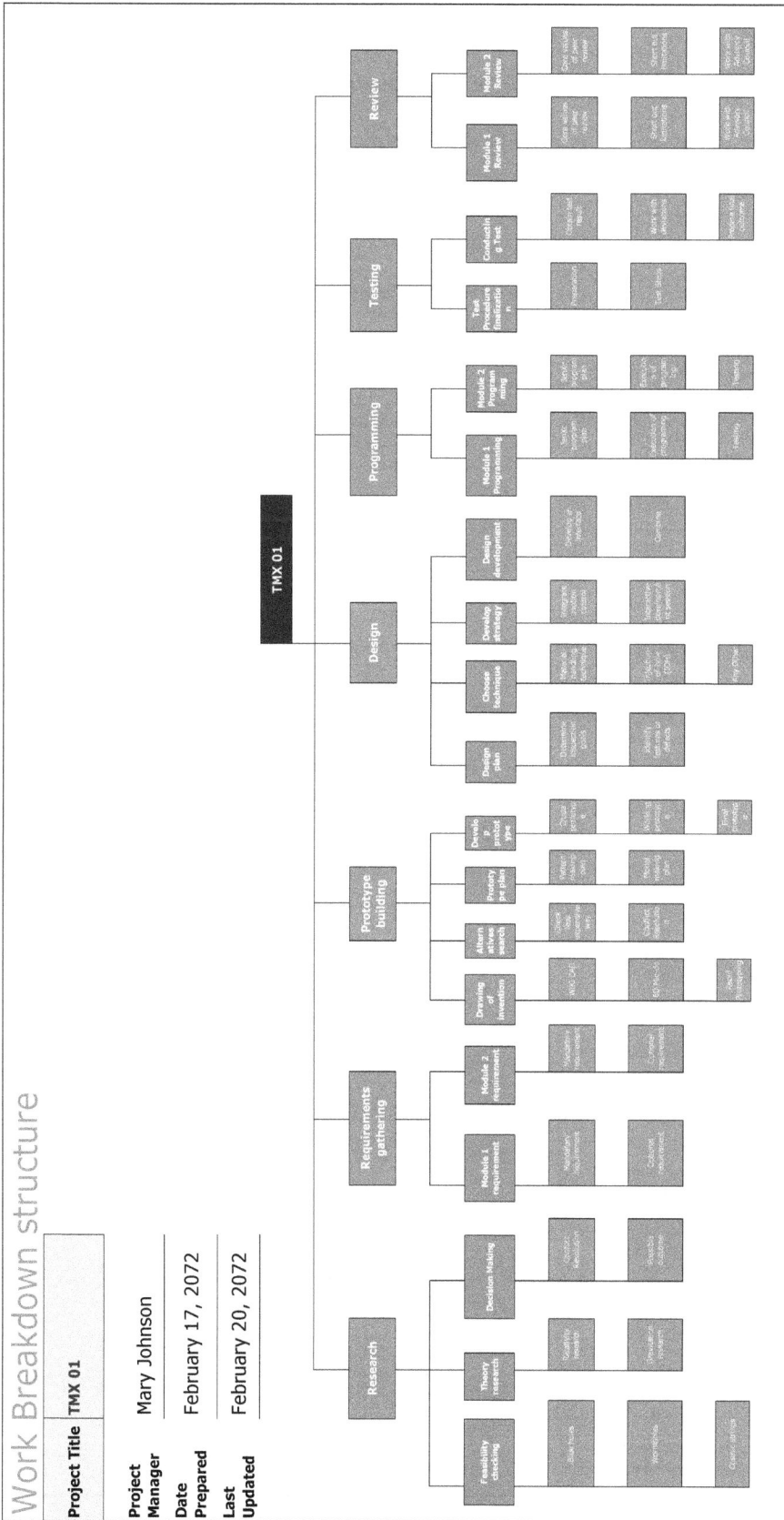

Form 9: **TXM01 WBS**

WBS Dictionary

WBS Dictionary

The WBS Dictionary is a companion document to the WBS in which the details of the components contained in the WBS are described.

WBS Dictionary

Project Title	TMX 01
Project Manager	Mary Johnson
Date Prepared	February 17, 2072
Last Updated	February 17, 2073

Work Package Name	Feasibility checking
Work Package ID	1.1

Description of the work		Use effective technique to verify the finite specification
Assigned to		Mike
Assumptions and constraints		Completion of activity by Year 2076
Schedule milestones		Research Complete
Resource requirement		Henry, Mike, Michael Mathieu, Ney Dimaculangan, Maria Aragon
Cost estimate		3500 million USD

Activity ID	Activity name	Activity cost
1.1.1	Blue holes	1450 million USD
1.1.2	Wormholes	1250 million USD
1.1.3	Cosmic strings	800 million USD

Acceptance criteria		Obtaining feasible decision
Quality requirements		N/A

Work Package Name	Theory research
Work Package ID	1.2

Description of the work		Study and compose creative work undertaken on a systematic basis
Assigned to		Oh Jin-Hyek
Assumptions and constraints		Completion of activity by Year 2076
Schedule milestones		Research Complete
Resource requirement		Alan Turing, Thyro Alfaro, Oh Jin-Hyek
Cost estimate		3400 million USD

Activity ID	Activity name	Activity cost
1.2.1	Relativity research	1700 million USD
1.2.2	Gravitation research	1700 million USD

Acceptance criteria		Obtaining feasible outcome
Quality requirements		N/A

WBS Dictionary

Work Package Name	Decision Making
Work Package ID	1.3

Description of the work		Test & work with similar related plans of conflicts and make decision
Assigned to		Mary Johnson
Assumptions and constraints		Completion of activity by Year 2076
Schedule milestones		Research Complete
Resource requirement		Mary Johnson, Michael Mathieu, Ney Dimaculangan
Cost estimate		300 million USD

Activity ID	Activity name	Activity cost
1.3.1	Conflict Resolution	200 million USD
1.3.2	Possible outcome	100 million USD

Acceptance criteria		Obtaining feasible outcome
Quality requirements		N/A

Work Package Name	Module 1 requirement
Work Package ID	2.1

Description of the work		Gather requirement that are actionable, measurable, testable, traceable with identified needs
Assigned to		Mary Johnson
Assumptions and constraints		Requirements finalized
Schedule milestones		Completion of activity by Year 2078
Resource requirement		Mary Johnson, Ney Dimaculangan, Maria Aragon
Cost estimate		700 million USD

Activity ID	Activity name	Activity cost
2.1.1	Mandatory requirement	400 million USD
2.1.2	Optional requirement	300 million USD

Acceptance criteria		Obtaining actionable, measurable, testable, traceable requirements
Quality requirements		N/A

WBS Dictionary

Work Package Name	Module 2 requirement
Work Package ID	2.2

Description of the work	Gather requirement that are actionable, measurable, testable, traceable, identified needs		
Assigned to	Mike		
Assumptions and constraints	Requirements finalized		
Schedule milestones	Completion of activity by Year 2078		
Resource requirement	Mike, Henry, Mike, Michael Mathieu		
Cost estimate	700 million USD		
	Activity ID	**Activity name**	**Activity cost**
	2.2.1	Mandatory requirement	400 million USD
	2.2.2	Optional requirement	300 million USD
Acceptance criteria	Obtaining actionable, measurable, testable, traceable requirements		
Quality requirements	N/A		

Work Package Name	Drawing of invention
Work Package ID	3.1

Description of the work	Analyze how to draw perspective views that show all the features of invention		
Assigned to	Max Planck		
Assumptions and constraints	Prototype built		
Schedule milestones	Completion of activity by Year 2080		
Resource requirement	Max Planck, Henry, Maria Aragon		
Cost estimate	2500 million USD		
	Activity ID	**Activity name**	**Activity cost**
	3.1.1	WiKi CAD	900 million USD
	3.1.2	6D Mic-do	500 million USD
	3.1.3	Rapid Prototyping	1100 million USD
Acceptance criteria	Successful analysis for the drawing of invention		
Quality requirements	As specified in quality management plan		

WBS Dictionary

Work Package Name	Alternatives search
Work Package ID	3.2

Description of the work	Search and finalize alternative and effective drawing method		
Assigned to	Mary Johnson		
Assumptions and constraints	Prototype built		
Schedule milestones	Completion of activity by Year 2080		
Resource requirement	Mary Johnson, Max Planck, Natalya Antyukh, Maria Aragon, Alan Turing		
Cost estimate	800 million USD		
	Activity ID	**Activity name**	**Activity cost**
	3.2.1	Check less expensive way	700 million USD
	3.2.2	Conflict Resolution	100 million USD
Acceptance criteria	Decision making for effective drawing method		
Quality requirements	N/A		

Work Package Name	Prototype plan
Work Package ID	3.3

Description of the work	Develop a blueprint plan to develop prototype		
Assigned to	Max Planck		
Assumptions and constraints	Prototype built		
Schedule milestones	Completion of activity by Year 2080		
Resource requirement	Max Planck, Natalya Antyukh, Maria Aragon, Alan Turing		
Cost estimate	2800 million USD		
	Activity ID	**Activity name**	**Activity cost**
	3.3.1	Pattern making plan	1000 million USD
	3.3.2	Model making plan	1800 million USD
Acceptance criteria	Blueprint plan development		
Quality requirements	As specified in quality management plan		

The WBS Dictionary:

• Provides an identification of the project deliverables and an elaborate description of the WBS components.

WBS Dictionary

Work Package Name	Develop prototype
Work Package ID	3.4

	Description of the work	Taking ideas and turning it into a tangible product
	Assigned to	Max Planck
	Assumptions and constraints	Prototype built
	Schedule milestones	Completion of activity by Year 2080
	Resource requirement	Henry, Natalya Antyukh, Maria Aragon
	Cost estimate	5800 million USD

Activity ID	Activity name	Activity cost
3.4.1	Crude prototype	1200 million USD
3.4.2	Working prototype	2400 million USD
3.4.3	Final prototype	2200 million USD

	Acceptance criteria	Prototype built
	Quality requirements	As specified in quality management plan

Work Package Name	Design plan
Work Package ID	4.1

	Description of the work	Develop the ways with the features and defects for designing
	Assigned to	Max Planck
	Assumptions and constraints	Developed design plan
	Schedule milestones	Design completed by Year 2083
	Resource requirement	Max Planck, Alan Turing
	Cost estimate	800 million USD

Activity ID	Activity name	Activity cost
4.1.1	Determine inspection goals	100 million USD
4.1.2	Identify features or defects	700 million USD

	Acceptance criteria	Design plan Development
	Quality requirements	N/A

WBS Dictionary

Work Package Name	Choose technique
Work Package ID	4.2

	Description of the work	Test and analyze best technique to design
	Assigned to	Max Planck
	Assumptions and constraints	Finalize design technique
	Schedule milestones	Design completed by Year 2083
	Resource requirement	Max Planck, Alan Turing, Henry
	Cost estimate	600 million USD

Activity ID	Activity name	Activity cost
4.2.1	Material-handling technique	100 million USD
4.2.2	Injection-of-hole (IOH)	200 million USD
4.2.3	Any Other	300 million USD

	Acceptance criteria	Identifying best technique
	Quality requirements	As specified in quality management plan

Work Package Name	Develop strategy
Work Package ID	4.3

	Description of the work	Develop a way to achieve design goals and reach success
	Assigned to	Mary Johnson
	Assumptions and constraints	Finalize design strategy
	Schedule milestones	Design completed by Year 2083
	Resource requirement	Mary Johnson, Alan Turing, Henry, Natalya Antyukh
	Cost estimate	1000 million USD

Activity ID	Activity name	Activity cost
4.3.1	Integrate motion control	500 million USD
4.3.2	Interactive development sessio	500 million USD

	Acceptance criteria	Feasible developed strategy
	Quality requirements	As specified in quality management plan

The WBS Dictionary:

- Describes the work in each WBS component that is required to produce the deliverables.

WBS Dictionary

Work Package Name	Design development
Work Package ID	4.4

Description of the work	Move design from the schematic phase to document developed design phase
Assigned to	Mary Johnson
Assumptions and constraints	Successful design development
Schedule milestones	Design completed by Year 2083
Resource requirement	Mary Johnson, Alan Turing, Henry, Natalya Antyukh, Maria Aragon
Cost estimate	7500 million USD

Activity ID	Activity name	Activity cost
4.4.1	Develop an interface	5000 million USD
4.4.2	Combine	2500 million USD

Acceptance criteria	Development of design
Quality requirements	As specified in quality management plan

Work Package Name	Module 1 Programming
Work Package ID	5.1

Description of the work	Develop language designed to communicate instructions
Assigned to	Tirunesh Dibaba
Assumptions and constraints	Successful programming
Schedule milestones	Programming done by year 2086
Resource requirement	Tirunesh Dibaba, Andrew, Maria Aragon
Cost estimate	9000 million USD

Activity ID	Activity name	Activity cost
5.1.1	JenXc program plan	500 million USD
5.1.2	Execution of program	7500 million USD
5.1.3	Testing	1000 million USD

Acceptance criteria	Develop successful programming
Quality requirements	As specified in quality management plan

WBS Dictionary

Work Package Name	Module 2 Programming
Work Package ID	5.2

Description of the work	Develop language designed to communicate instructions
Assigned to	Tirunesh Dibaba
Assumptions and constraints	Successful programming
Schedule milestones	Programming done by year 2086
Resource requirement	Tirunesh Dibaba, Sally Pearson, Maria Aragon
Cost estimate	9000 million USD

Activity ID	Activity name	Activity cost
5.2.1	JenXc program plan	500 million USD
5.2.2	Execution of programing	7500 million USD
5.2.3	Testing	1000 million USD

Acceptance criteria	Develop successful programming
Quality requirements	As specified in quality management plan

Work Package Name	Test procedure finalization
Work Package ID	6.1

Description of the work	Develop best suited procedure for testing
Assigned to	Oh Jin-Hyek
Assumptions and constraints	Test procedure finalization
Schedule milestones	Testing done by year 2087
Resource requirement	Oh Jin-Hyek, Henry, Alan Turing
Cost estimate	600 million USD

Activity ID	Activity name	Activity cost
6.1.1	Preparation	100 million USD
6.1.2	Test Steps	500 million USD

Acceptance criteria	Finalization test procedure
Quality requirements	As specified in quality management plan

Descriptions included in the WBS Dictionary include: work packages, control accounts, code of account identifiers, cost estimates, resource information, project schedule and dependencies.

WBS Dictionary

Work Package Name	Conducting Test
Work Package ID	6.2

	Description of the work	Continuously records machine heart's rhythms and work for defects
	Assigned to	Oh Jin-Hyek
	Assumptions and constraints	Successfully conduct machine test
	Schedule milestones	Testing done by year 2087
	Resource requirement	Oh Jin-Hyek, Henry, Alan Turing
	Cost estimate	3100 million USD

Activity ID	Activity name	Activity cost
6.2.1	Obtain test result	100 million USD
6.2.2	Work with deviations	2800 million USD
6.2.3	Prepare final outcome	200 million USD

	Acceptance criteria	Successful test result
	Quality requirements	As specified in quality management plan

Work Package Name	Module 1 Review
Work Package ID	7.1

	Description of the work	Analyze settings, prices, pros and cons of machines
	Assigned to	Mike
	Assumptions and constraints	Valued review
	Schedule milestones	Phase End Review complete by year 2088
	Resource requirement	Natalya Antyukh, Mike, Thyro Alfaro
	Cost estimate	450 million USD

Activity ID	Activity name	Activity cost
7.1.1	Core values of peer review	200 million USD
7.1.2	Short out limitations	150 million USD
7.1.3	Work with Advisory Council	100 million USD

	Acceptance criteria	Finalization of review
	Quality requirements	As specified in quality management plan

WBS Dictionary

Work Package Name	Module 2 Review
Work Package ID	7.2

	Description of the work	Analyze settings, prices, pros and cons of machines
	Assigned to	Mary Johnson
	Assumptions and constraints	Valued review
	Schedule milestones	Phase End Review complete by year 2088
	Resource requirement	Mary Johnson, Mike, Ney Dimaculangan, Michael Mathieu
	Cost estimate	450 million USD

Activity ID	Activity name	Activity cost
7.2.1	Core values of peer review	200 million USD
7.2.2	Short out limitations	150 million USD
7.2.3	Work with Advisory Council	100 million USD

	Acceptance criteria	Finalization of review
	Quality requirements	As specified in quality management plan

Form 10: TXM01 WBS Dictionary

Scope Baseline

The scope baseline is made up of the approved Project Scope Statement, the Work Breakdown Structure (WBS) and WBS Dictionary.

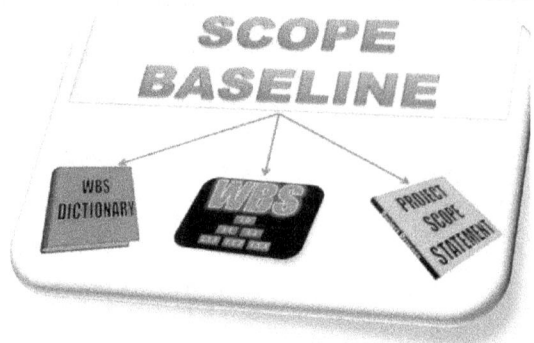

8. Plan Schedule Management

Plan Schedule Management involves developing a plan for how time will be managed on the project, and how the schedule will be developed. In the world of the PMI, always plan first before taking action. Whatever the Knowledge Area, create a plan first and then execute it.

In this process, the team establishes the protocol, policies, procedures, and guidelines for developing, managing and controlling the schedule. This is where the team should intentionally plan how to develop a good schedule, with precise and realistic targets.

Inputs	Tools and Techniques	Outputs
○ Project management plan ○ Project charter ○ Enterprise environmental factors ○ Organizational process assets	○ Expert judgment ○ Analytical techniques ○ Meetings	○ Schedule management plan

Figure 11: Plan Schedule Management: Inputs, Tools & Techniques and Outputs

Schedule Management Plan

A schedule management plan is a strategic and intentional plan for how the schedule will be developed and managed. It could be detailed or high level. It could be very broad or brief depending on the size of the project, but ultimately you should think about aspects such as; how to define, assess and update the schedule. The Schedule Management Plan contains information used to guide time management activities.

Schedule Management Plan

Project Title:	TMX 01		

Project Sponsor:	Alfred Pinkus and Jonny Roberts	Date Prepared:	28-Apr-73
Project	Mary Johnson	Project	Professor Zakari

Purpose

The Schedule Management Plan is the roadmap for how to define activities, sequence activities in order, estimate resources and duration, develop the schedule and control the schedule; preventing unauthorized extensions and schedule delays. It also documents the process for managing schedule changes.

Schedule Management Procedure and Approaches

Mary Johnson together with the project team member and Alfred Pinkus & Jonny Roberts will ensure that the schedule is developed following the 7 standard PMI project mnagement processes for schedule management. The PM will ensure all schedule risks are identified, analyzed, and managed throughout the life cycle of the TMX 01 project.

Defining Activities

The project management team and selected stakeholders will be involved to decompose the WBS work-packages in order to adequately define activities and activity attributes. The 100% rule should apply. In instances where applicable, rolling-wave planning may be used. Refer to OPA rules for Rolling Wave Planning in organizational databases.

Estimating the Schedule Resources, Durations and Developing the Schedule

* The schedule estinates will be developed using a combination of estimating methods as the project transitions from phase to phase but ideally, bottom-up estimating should be used by the project team wherever possible.

* The project team should use the most skilled resources available regardless cost from internal sources or external agencies and sister-organizations.

* The project team should use the most superior strength, grades and accurate material and equipment resources available from partners and verified vendors in the VMS.

* Acceptable range for determining activity durations: -5% to 5%

* Units of measure to be used (hours, days, months or weeks): Months

* Project schedule model maintenance: Weekly schedule updates required

* Earned value measurement rules: percent complete and weighted milestone methods.

* The project team must provide a network diagram and level 2 schedule for inclusion in the greater program. This will be different from the project schedule.

* Team members should provide the rationale for all conclusions and estimates derived to the PM.

* Historical information from similar Defense and Space projects should be used where applicable.

* Schedule activities should roll up appropriately to Work Packages and Control Accounts for EVM Analysis and Tracking using the EVMS.

Project Manager Signature		Sponsor or Originator Signature	

Project Manager Name		Sponsor or Originator Name	
Date		Date	

Form 11: Schedule Management Plan

9. Define Activities

Defining activities is done by breaking down the lowest level of the WBS (work package) into smaller, more manageable pieces called activities or tasks. It involves:

- Identifying the lowest level in the WBS (work package) which provides a basis for estimating.
- Further decomposing work packages into schedule activities.
- Defining the activities that must occur to achieve the project's end result and deliverables in detail.
- Identifying and documenting the work to be performed.

Inputs	Tools and Techniques	Outputs
◌ Schedule management plan ◌ Scope baseline ◌ Enterprise environmental factors ◌ Organizational process assets	◌ Decomposition ◌ Rolling wave planning ◌ Expert judgment	◌ Activity list ◌ Activity attributes ◌ Milestone list

Figure 12: Define Activities: Inputs, Tools & Techniques and Outputs

Activity List

An activity list is a list of all schedule activities to be performed on a project and a scope of work description of each in suitable detail to ensure the Project Team members understand it. Activities consist of work or effort required to complete a work package and ultimately, a deliverable. Project work can be estimated, scheduled, executed, monitored and controlled at the activity level.

Activity List

Project Title	TMX 01

Project Manager	Mary Johnson
Date Prepared	February 18, 2073
Last Updated	February 18, 2073

WBS Code	Activity List	Description
1.1.1	Blue holes	A blue hole is a region of space time invented in 2027 in which gravity prevents anything, including light from escaping. The activity involves the study and research of application of blue holes for TMX 01 machine.
1.1.2	Wormholes	Wormholes create shortcuts for long journeys across the universe using the theory of relativity. Research ensures to bring wormholes from dangers of sudden collapse, high radiation and dangerous contact with exotic matter.
1.1.3	Cosmic strings	As proven at 2030, Cosmic strings, the one dimensional topological defects form during a symmetry breaking phase transition when the topology of the vacuum manifold associated. Study will ensure at least one string per Hubble volume to be formed.
1.2.1	Relativity research	The activity will ensure research including cosmology and general relativity.
1.2.2	Gravitation research	The research will ensure graviton to be massless as gravitational force will be appear having unlimited range with twice spin boson.
1.3.1	Conflict Resolution	Activity will resolve all the conflicts related to the research and study for TMX 01.
1.3.2	Possible outcome	The activity will formalize possible outcome of all research and conflict as shown in implementing the machine.
2.1.1	Mandatory requirement (Module- 1)	The requirements will include all the mandatory elements from large Hardron Collider or a rocket to all the technical, natural elements available or possible be built Forward time travel.
2.1.2	Optional requirement (Module- 1)	The requirements will include all the optional elements from large Hardron Collider or a rocket to all the technical, natural elements available or possible be build Forward time travel.
2.2.1	Mandatory requirement (Module- 2)	The requirements will include all the optional elements from large Hardron Collider or a rocket to all the technical, natural elements available or possible be built Forward time travel.
2.2.2	Optional requirement (Module- 2)	The requirements will include all the optional elements from large Hardron Collider or a rocket to all the technical, natural elements available or possible be build Backward time travel.
3.1.1	WiKi CAD	Develop plan on how to draw perspective views through Wiki CAD that show all the features of invention
3.1.2	6D Mic-do	Develop a plan on how to draw perspective views through 6D Mic-do that show all the features of invention
3.1.3	Rapid Prototyping	Develop a plan on how to draw perspective views through Rapid Prototyping that show all the features of invention
3.2.1	Check less expensive way	Search alternative and cost effective drawing method
3.2.2	Conflict Resolution	Finalize most effective drawing method after resolving conflict.
3.3.1	Pattern making plan	Develop a blueprint Pattern making plan to develop prototype.
3.3.2	Model making plan	Develop a blueprint Model making plan to develop prototype.
3.4.1	Crude prototype	Work on establish a Crude prototype
3.4.2	Working prototype	Work on establish a Working prototype
3.4.3	Final prototype	Work on establish Final prototype
4.1.1	Determine inspection goals	Determine and finalize inspection goals for design plan
4.1.2	Identify features or defects	Identify features or defects for design plan
4.2.1	Material-handling technique	Test and analyze Material-handling technique to design
4.2.2	Injection-of-hole (IOH)	Test and analyze Injection-of-hole (IOH) technique to design
4.2.3	Any Other	Search & Test any other advanced technique to design
4.3.1	Integrate motion control	Use integrate motion control to develop a way to achieve design goals and reach success
4.3.2	Interactive development session	Work on interactive development session to develop a way to achieve design goals and reach success
4.4.1	Develop an interface	Work on developed design phase to Develop an interface
4.4.2	Combine	Combine and mix developed elements to finalize design development
5.1.1	JenXc program plan (module-1)	Work on JenXc program plan for machine 1 programing
5.1.2	Execution of programing (module-1)	Work on programming to enable machine to be able to Forward time travel
5.1.3	Testing (module-1)	Test on various methods available to measure and deviation on module 1
5.2.1	JenXc program plan (module-2)	Work on JenXc program plan for machine 2 programing

Form 12: Activity List

Activity Attributes

An activity attribute is an extension of an activity description which further identifies the activity and aids in organizing and planning the activity. Examples: activity ID, WBS ID, activity name, activity codes, description, identifiers, codes, predecessor and successor information, logical relationships and imposed dates

Activity Attributes

Project Title		TMX 01	
Project Manager		Mary Johnson	
Date Prepared		February 15, 2073	
Last Updated		February 22, 2073	

Activity ID	Activity Name		WBS ID
1.1.1	Blue holes		1.1
Activity Description			
A blue hole is a region of space time invented in 2027 from which gravity prevents anything, including light from escaping. The activity involves study and research for application of blue holes for TMX 01 machine.			
Responsibility	Mike		
Resource requirement	Henry, Mike, Michael Mathieu, Mecha-Streisand		
Predecessors	Start	Relationship	FS
Successor	1.2.1, 1.2.2	Relationship	FS
Activity Type	Fixed duration activity of 10 months		
Location	Noveau Inconnu Lab		
Assumption	Completion of activity by Year 2076		
Constraint	Activity has budget of 1450 million USD		

Activity ID	Activity Name		WBS ID
1.1.2	Wormholes		1.1
Activity Description			
Wormholes create shortcuts for long journeys across the universe using the theory of relativity. Research will ensure to bring wormholes from dangers of sudden collapse, high radiation and dangerous contact with exotic matter.			
Responsibility	Mike		
Resource requirement	Mike, Ney Dimaculangan, Maria Aragon, Grinders-MX52.3		
Predecessors	Start	Relationship	FS
Successor	1.2.1, 1.2.2	Relationship	FS
Activity Type	Fixed duration activity of 8 months		
Location	Noveau Inconnu Lab		
Assumption	Completion of activity by Year 2076		
Constraint	Activity has budget of 1250 million USD		

Activity Attributes

Activity ID	Activity Name		WBS ID
1.2.1	Relativity research		1.2
Activity Description			

The active will ensure research including cosmology and general relativity.

Responsibility	Oh Jin-Hyek		
Resource requirement	Michael Mathieu, Oh Jin-Hyek, Thyro Alfaro, Jack-bots300		
Predecessors	1.1.1, 1.1.2, 1.1.:	Relationship	FS
Successor	1.3.1	Relationship	FS
Activity Type	Fixed duration activity		
Location	Noveau Inconnu Lab		
Assumption	Completion of activity by Year 2076		
Constraint	Activity has budget of 1700 million USD		

Activity ID	Activity Name		WBS ID
1.2.2	Gravitation research		1.2
Activity Description			

The research will ensure graviton to be massless as gravitational force will be appear having unlimited range with twice spin boson.

Responsibility	Oh Jin-Hyek		
Resource requirement	Oh Jin-Hyek, Thyro Alfaro, Galactus Robote		
Predecessors	1.1.1, 1.1.2, 1.1.:	Relationship	FS
Successor	1.3.1	Relationship	FS
Activity Type	Fixed duration activity		
Location	Noveau Inconnu Lab		
Assumption	Completion of activity by Year 2076		
Constraint	Activity has budget of 1700 million USD		

Activity ID	Activity Name		WBS ID
1.3.1	Conflict Resolution		1.3
Activity Description			

Activity will resolve all the conflicts related to the research and study for TMX 01.

Responsibility	Mary Johnson		
Resource requirement	Oh Jin-Hyek, Mary Johnson, Krybots5TmXC		
Predecessors	1.2.1, 1.2.2	Relationship	FS
Successor	1.3.2	Relationship	FS
Activity Type	Fixed duration activity		
Location	Noveau Inconnu office		
Assumption	Completion of activity by Year 2076		
Constraint	Activity has budget of 200 million USD		

Activity Attributes

Activity ID	Activity Name	WBS ID
1.3.2	Possible outcome	1.3

Activity Description

The activity will formalize possible outcome of all research and conflict as show way to implement the machine.

Responsibility	Mary Johnson	
Resource requirement	Oh Jin-Hyek, Mary Johnson, Lab	
Predecessors	1.2.2	Relationship	FS
Successor	2.1.1	Relationship	FS
Activity Type	Fixed duration activity	
Location	Noveau Inconnu Office	
Assumption	Completion of activity by Year 2076	
Constraint	Activity has budget of 100 million USD	

Activity ID	Activity Name	WBS ID
2.1.1	Mandatory requirement (Module- 1)	2.1

Activity Description

The requirements will include all the mandatory elements from large Hardron Collider or a rocket to all the technical, natural elements available or possible be built Forward time travel.

Responsibility	Mary Johnson	
Resource requirement	Mary Johnson, Thyro Alfaro, Trin-E through Zu-Zana	
Predecessors	1.3.2	Relationship	FS
Successor	2.1.2, 2.2.1	Relationship	FS
Activity Type	Fixed duration activity	
Location	Noveau Inconnu Lab	
Assumption	Completion of activity by Year 2078	
Constraint	Activity has budget of 400 million USD	

Activity ID	Activity Name	WBS ID
2.1.2	Optional requirement (Module- 1)	2.1

Activity Description

The requirements will include all the optional elements from large Hardron Collider or a rocket to all the technical, natural elements available or possible be build Forward time travel.

Responsibility	Mary Johnson	
Resource requirement	Mary Johnson, Ney Dimaculangan, Interactive Canine	
Predecessors	2.1.1	Relationship	FS
Successor	2.2.2	Relationship	FF
Activity Type	Fixed duration activity	
Location	Noveau Inconnu Lab	
Assumption	Completion of activity by Year 2078	
Constraint	Activity has budget of 300 million USD	

Activity Attributes

Activity ID	Activity Name	WBS ID
2.2.1	Mandatory requirement (Module- 2)	2.2

Activity Description

The requirements will include all the optional elements from large Hardron Collider or a rocket to all the technical, natural elements available or possible be built Forward time travel.

Responsibility	Mary Johnson	
Resource requirement	Mike, Mary Johnson, Trin-E through Zu-Zana	
Predecessors	2.1.2	Relationship	FS
Successor	2.2.2	Relationship	FF
Activity Type	Fixed duration activity	
Location	Noveau Inconnu Lab	
Assumption	Completion of activity by Year 2078	
Constraint	Activity has budget of 400 million USD	

Activity ID	Activity Name	WBS ID
2.2.2	Optional requirement (Module- 2)	2.2

Activity Description

The requirements will include all the optional elements from large Hardron Collider or a rocket to all the technical, natural elements available or possible be build Backward time travel.

Responsibility	Mary Johnson	
Resource requirement	Mary Johnson, Ney Dimaculangan, Interactive Canine	
Predecessors	2.1.2, 2.2.1	Relationship	FF
Successor	3.1.1, 3.1.2, 3.1..	Relationship	FS
Activity Type	Fixed duration activity	
Location	Noveau Inconnu Lab	
Assumption	Completion of activity by Year 2078	
Constraint	Activity has budget of 300 million USD	

Activity ID	Activity Name	WBS ID
3.1.1	WiKi CAD	3.1

Activity Description

Develop plan on how to draw perspective views through WiKi CAD that show all the features of invention

Responsibility	Max Planck	
Resource requirement	Max Planck, Maria Aragon, SILKY(MMF108-41)	
Predecessors	2.2.2	Relationship	FS
Successor	3.2.1	Relationship	FS
Activity Type	Fixed duration activity	
Location	Noveau Inconnu Lab	
Assumption	Completion of activity by Year 2080	
Constraint	Activity has budget of 900 million USD	

Activity Attributes

Activity ID	Activity Name	WBS ID
3.1.2	6D Mic-do	3.1

Activity Description

Develop plan on how to draw perspective views through 6D Mic-do that show all the features of invention

Responsibility	Max Planck	
Resource requirement	Max Planck, Maria Aragon, Mary Johnson, Mahoro-20H	
Predecessors	2.2.2	Relationship	FS
Successor	3.2.1	Relationship	FS
Activity Type	Fixed duration activity	
Location	Noveau Inconnu Lab	
Assumption	Completion of activity by Year 2080	
Constraint	Activity has budget of 500 million USD	

Activity ID	Activity Name	WBS ID
3.1.3	Rapid Prototyping	3.1

Activity Description

Develop plan on how to draw perspective views through Rapid Prototyping that show all the features of invention

Responsibility	Max Planck	
Resource requirement	Mary Johnson, Max Planck, Sasquatch switch	
Predecessors	2.2.2	Relationship	FS
Successor	3.2.1	Relationship	FS
Activity Type	Fixed duration activity	
Location	Noveau Inconnu Lab	
Assumption	Completion of activity by Year 2080	
Constraint	Activity has budget of 1100 million USD	

Activity ID	Activity Name	WBS ID
3.2.1	Check less expensive way	3.2

Activity Description

Search alternative and cost effective drawing method

Responsibility	Mary Johnson	
Resource requirement	Mary Johnson, Max Planck, Ney Dimaculangan, Fin Fang Foom_ModDn	
Predecessors	3.1.1, 3.1.2, 3.1..	Relationship	FS
Successor	3.2.2	Relationship	FS
Activity Type	Fixed duration activity	
Location	Noveau Inconnu Lab	
Assumption	Completion of activity by Year 2080	
Constraint	Activity has budget of 700 million USD	

Activity Attributes

Activity ID	Activity Name	WBS ID
3.2.2	Conflict Resolution	3.2

Activity Description

Finalize most effective drawing method after resolving conflict.

Responsibility	Mary Johnson	
Resource requirement	Max Planck, Mary Johnson, Lab	
Predecessors	3.2.1	Relationship	FS
Successor	3.3.1, 3.3.2	Relationship	FS
Activity Type	Fixed duration activity	
Location	Noveau Inconnu office	
Assumption	Completion of activity by Year 2080	
Constraint	Activity has budget of 100 million USD	

Activity ID	Activity Name	WBS ID
3.3.1	Pattern making plan	3.3

Activity Description

Develop a blueprint Pattern making plan to develop prototype.

Responsibility	Max Planck	
Resource requirement	Max Planck, Ney Dimaculangan, Simulacron-35	
Predecessors	3.2.2	Relationship	FS
Successor	3.4.1	Relationship	FS
Activity Type	Fixed duration activity	
Location	Noveau Inconnu Lab	
Assumption	Completion of activity by Year 2080	
Constraint	Activity has budget of 1000 million USD	

Activity ID	Activity Name	WBS ID
3.3.2	Model making plan	3.3

Activity Description

Develop a blueprint Model making plan to develop prototype.

Responsibility	Max Planck	
Resource requirement	Alan Turing, Max Planck, Weather-controlling robot	
Predecessors	3.2.2	Relationship	FS
Successor	3.4.1	Relationship	FS
Activity Type	Fixed duration activity	
Location	Noveau Inconnu Lab	
Assumption	Completion of activity by Year 2080	
Constraint	Activity has budget of 1800 million USD	

Activity Attributes

Activity ID	Activity Name	WBS ID
3.4.1	Crude prototype	3.4

Activity Description

Work on establish a Crude prototype

Responsibility	Max Planck	
Resource requirement	Alan Turing, Max Planck, Rocket Raccoon_white32	
Predecessors	3.3.1, 3.3.2	Relationship	FS
Successor	3.4.2	Relationship	FS
Activity Type	Fixed duration activity	
Location	Noveau Inconnu Lab	
Assumption	Completion of activity by Year 2080	
Constraint	Activity has budget of 1200 million USD	

Activity ID	Activity Name	WBS ID
3.4.2	Working prototype	3.4

Activity Description

Work on establish a Working prototype

Responsibility	Max Planck	
Resource requirement	Michael Mathieu, Max Planck, HAL 9000_TC	
Predecessors	3.4.1	Relationship	FS
Successor	3.4.3	Relationship	FS
Activity Type	Fixed duration activity	
Location	Noveau Inconnu Lab	
Assumption	Completion of activity by Year 2080	
Constraint	Activity has budget of 2400 million USD	

Activity ID	Activity Name	WBS ID
3.4.3	Final prototype	3.4

Activity Description

Work on establish Final prototype

Responsibility	Max Planck	
Resource requirement	Max Planck, Mary Johnson, Rorschach robote 2050MX	
Predecessors	3.4.2	Relationship	FS
Successor	4.1.1	Relationship	FF
Activity Type	Fixed duration activity	
Location	Noveau Inconnu Lab	
Assumption	Completion of activity by Year 2080	
Constraint	Activity has budget of 2200 million USD	

Activity Attributes

Activity ID	Activity Name	WBS ID
4.1.1	Determine inspection goals	4.1

Activity Description

Determine and finalize inspection goals for design plan

Responsibility	Max Planck	
Resource requirement	Max Planck, Mike, Interactive Canine	
Predecessors	4.1.1	Relationship	FS
Successor	2, 4.2.1, 4.2.2, 4	Relationship	FS
Activity Type	Fixed duration activity	
Location	Noveau Inconnu Lab	
Assumption	Completion of activity by Year 2083	
Constraint	Activity has budget of 100 million USD	

Activity ID	Activity Name	WBS ID
4.1.2	Identify features or defects	4.1

Activity Description

Identify features or defects for design plan

Responsibility	Max Planck	
Resource requirement	Max Planck, Mike, replicators	
Predecessors	4.4.1	Relationship	FS
Successor	4.2.1	Relationship	FF
Activity Type	Fixed duration activity	
Location	Noveau Inconnu Lab	
Assumption	Completion of activity by Year 2083	
Constraint	Activity has budget of 700 million USD	

Activity ID	Activity Name	WBS ID
4.2.1	Material-handling technique	4.2

Activity Description

Test and analyze Material-handling technique to design

Responsibility	Max Planck	
Resource requirement	Max Planck, Mike, robotic vampire	
Predecessors	4.1.1	Relationship	SS
Successor	4.3.1	Relationship	FS
Activity Type	Fixed duration activity	
Location	Noveau Inconnu Lab	
Assumption	Completion of activity by Year 2083	
Constraint	Activity has budget of 100 million USD	

Activity Attributes

Activity ID	Activity Name	WBS ID
4.2.2	Injection-of-hole (IOH)	4.2

Activity Description

Test and analyze Injection-of-hole (IOH) technique to design

Responsibility	Max Planck	
Resource requirement	Max Planck, Mike, Müller-Fokker tapes	
Predecessors	4.1.1	Relationship	FS
Successor	4.3.1	Relationship	FS
Activity Type	Fixed duration activity	
Location	Noveau Inconnu Lab	
Assumption	Completion of activity by Year 2083	
Constraint	Activity has budget of 200 million USD	

Activity ID	Activity Name	WBS ID
4.2.3	Any Other	4.2

Activity Description

Search & Test any other advanced technique to design

Responsibility	Max Planck	
Resource requirement	Max Planck, Mike, Reserve for future technogy	
Predecessors	4.1.1	Relationship	FS
Successor	4.3.1	Relationship	FS
Activity Type	Fixed duration activity	
Location	Noveau Inconnu Lab	
Assumption	Completion of activity by Year 2083	
Constraint	Activity has budget of 300 million USD	

Activity ID	Activity Name	WBS ID
4.3.1	Integrate motion control	4.3

Activity Description

Use integrate motion control to develop a way to achieve design goals and reach success

Responsibility	Mary Johnson	
Resource requirement	Max Planck, Mary Johnson, Aqua Hunger Force Controller	
Predecessors	.2.1, 4.2.2, 4.2..	Relationship	FS
Successor	4.3.2	Relationship	FS
Activity Type	Fixed duration activity	
Location	Noveau Inconnu Lab	
Assumption	Completion of activity by Year 2083	
Constraint	Activity has budget of 500 million USD	

Activity Attributes

Activity ID	Activity Name	WBS ID
4.3.2	Interactive development session	4.3

Activity Description

Work on interactive development session to develop a way to achieve design goals and reach success

Responsibility	Mary Johnson	
Resource requirement	Max Planck, Mary Johnson, Aqua Hunger Force Controller	
Predecessors	4.3.1	Relationship	FS
Successor	4.4.1	Relationship	FS
Activity Type	Fixed duration activity	
Location	Noveau Inconnu Lab	
Assumption	Completion of activity by Year 2083	
Constraint	Activity has budget of 500 million USD	

Activity ID	Activity Name	WBS ID
4.4.1	Develop an interface	4.4

Activity Description

Work on developed design phase to Develop an interface

Responsibility	Mary Johnson	
Resource requirement	Max Planck, Mary Johnson, Alan Turing, Henry, Titans52Q, Lab, TMT_IN	
Predecessors	4.3.2	Relationship	FS
Successor	4.4.2	Relationship	FS
Activity Type	Fixed duration activity	
Location	Noveau Inconnu Lab	
Assumption	Completion of activity by Year 2083	
Constraint	Activity has budget of 5000 million USD	

Activity ID	Activity Name	WBS ID
4.4.2	Combine	4.4

Activity Description

Combine and mix developed elements to finalize design development

Responsibility	Mary Johnson	
Resource requirement	Mary Johnson, Alan Turing, Henry, Lab, TMT_IN	
Predecessors	4.4.1	Relationship	FS
Successor	5.1.1	Relationship	FS
Activity Type	Fixed duration activity	
Location	Noveau Inconnu Lab	
Assumption	Completion of activity by Year 2083	
Constraint	Activity has budget of 2500 million USD	

Activity Attributes

Activity ID	Activity Name	WBS ID
5.1.1	JenXc program plan (module-1)	5.1

Activity Description		
Work on JenXc program plan for machine 1 programing		

Responsibility	Tirunesh Dibaba	
Resource requirement	Tirunesh Dibaba, Sally Pearson, Processor Hyper Intelligent Encriptor	
Predecessors	4.4.2	Relationship	FS
Successor	5.1.2, 5.2.1	Relationship	FS, FF
Activity Type	Fixed duration activity	
Location	Noveau Inconnu Lab	
Assumption	Completion of activity by Year 2086	
Constraint	Activity has budget of 500 million USD	

Activity ID	Activity Name	WBS ID
5.1.2	Execution of programing (module-1)	5.1

Activity Description		
Work on programming to enable machine to be able to Forward time travel		

Responsibility	Tirunesh Dibaba	
Resource requirement	Tirunesh Dibaba, Natalya Antyukh, Andrew, HMX-17b Milfa_DU	
Predecessors	5.1.1	Relationship	FS
Successor	5.1.3	Relationship	FS
Activity Type	Fixed duration activity	
Location	Noveau Inconnu Lab	
Assumption	Completion of activity by Year 2086	
Constraint	Activity has budget of 7500 million USD	

Activity ID	Activity Name	WBS ID
5.1.3	Testing (module-1)	5.1

Activity Description		
Test on various methods available to measure and deviation on module 1		

Responsibility	Tirunesh Dibaba	
Resource requirement	Tirunesh Dibaba, Natalya Antyukh, Andrew, Simulacron-35	
Predecessors	5.1.2	Relationship	FS
Successor	5.2.3	Relationship	FF
Activity Type	Fixed duration activity	
Location	Noveau Inconnu Lab	
Assumption	Completion of activity by Year 2086	
Constraint	Activity has budget of 1000 million USD	

Activity Attributes

Activity ID	Activity Name	WBS ID
5.2.1	JenXc program plan (module-2)	5.2

Activity Description		
Work on JenXc program plan for machine 2 programing		

Responsibility	Tirunesh Dibaba	
Resource requirement	Tirunesh Dibaba, Sally Pearson, Processor Hyper Intelligent Encriptor	
Predecessors	5.1.1	Relationship	FF
Successor	5.2.2	Relationship	FS
Activity Type	Fixed duration activity	
Location	Noveau Inconnu Lab	
Assumption	Completion of activity by Year 2086	
Constraint	Activity has budget of 500 million USD	

Activity ID	Activity Name	WBS ID
5.2.2	Execution of programing (module-2)	5.2

Activity Description		
Work on programming to enable machine to be able to Backward time travel		

Responsibility	Tirunesh Dibaba	
Resource requirement	Tirunesh Dibaba, Sally Pearson, Natalya Antyukh, HMX-17c Shilfa_DU	
Predecessors	5.2.1	Relationship	FS
Successor	5.2.3	Relationship	FS
Activity Type	Fixed duration activity	
Location	Noveau Inconnu Lab	
Assumption	Completion of activity by Year 2086	
Constraint	Activity has budget of 7500 million USD	

Activity ID	Activity Name	WBS ID
5.2.3	Testing (module-2)	5.2

Activity Description		
Test on various methods available to measure and deviation on module 2		

Responsibility	Tirunesh Dibaba	
Resource requirement	Tirunesh Dibaba, , Natalya Antyukh, Andrew, Simulacron-35	
Predecessors	5.2.2, 5.1.3	Relationship	FS, FF
Successor	6.1.1	Relationship	FS
Activity Type	Fixed duration activity	
Location	Noveau Inconnu Lab	
Assumption	Completion of activity by Year 2086	
Constraint	Activity has budget of 1000 million USD	

Activity Attributes

Activity ID	Activity Name	WBS ID
6.1.1	Preparation	6.1

Activity Description		
Take necessary preparation to work on test procedure		

Responsibility	Oh Jin-Hyek	
Resource requirement	Maria Aragon,Oh Jin-Hyek, Lab	
Predecessors	5.2.3	Relationship	FS
Successor	6.1.2	Relationship	FS
Activity Type	Fixed duration activity	
Location	Noveau Inconnu Lab	
Assumption	Completion of activity by Year 2087	
Constraint	Activity has budget of 100 million USD	

Activity ID	Activity Name	WBS ID
6.1.2	Test Steps	6.1

Activity Description		
Finalize test procedure after resolving conflict		

Responsibility	Oh Jin-Hyek	
Resource requirement	Oh Jin-Hyek, Mary Johnson, Processor Hyper Intelligent Encriptor	
Predecessors	6.1.1	Relationship	FS
Successor	6.2.1	Relationship	FS
Activity Type	Fixed duration activity	
Location	Noveau Inconnu Lab	
Assumption	Completion of activity by Year 2087	
Constraint	Activity has budget of 500 million USD	

Activity ID	Activity Name	WBS ID
6.2.1	Obtain test result	6.2

Activity Description		
Obtain test results and valid data		

Responsibility	Oh Jin-Hyek	
Resource requirement	Oh Jin-Hyek, Mary Johnson, Lab, tester	
Predecessors	6.1.2	Relationship	FS
Successor	6.2.2	Relationship	FS
Activity Type	Fixed duration activity	
Location	Noveau Inconnu Lab	
Assumption	Completion of activity by Year 2087	
Constraint	Activity has budget of 100 million USD	

Activity Attributes

Activity ID	Activity Name	WBS ID
6.2.2	Work with deviations	6.2

Activity Description		
Work on deviation and fix the problem by inspection		

Responsibility	Oh Jin-Hyek	
Resource requirement	Oh Jin-Hyek, Mary Johnson, Maria Aragon, Lab, Simulacron-35, CCO	
Predecessors	6.2.1	Relationship	FS
Successor	6.2.3	Relationship	FS
Activity Type	Fixed duration activity	
Location	Noveau Inconnu Lab	
Assumption	Completion of activity by Year 2087	
Constraint	Activity has budget of 2800 million USD	

Activity ID	Activity Name	WBS ID
6.2.3	Prepare final outcome	6.2

Activity Description		
Work on final outcome of the modules		

Responsibility	Oh Jin-Hyek	
Resource requirement	Oh Jin-Hyek, Mary Johnson, Interactive Canine, Lab	
Predecessors	6.2.2	Relationship	FS
Successor	7.1.1	Relationship	FS
Activity Type	Fixed duration activity	
Location	Noveau Inconnu Lab	
Assumption	Completion of activity by Year 2087	
Constraint	Activity has budget of 200 million USD	

Activity ID	Activity Name	WBS ID
7.1.1	Core values of peer review	7.1

Activity Description		
Analyze settings for module 1 by core values of peer review		

Responsibility	Mike	
Resource requirement	Henry, Ney Dimaculangan, Mike, TMTX2050 robote	
Predecessors	6.2.3	Relationship	FS
Successor	7.1.2, 7.2.1	Relationship	FS
Activity Type	Fixed duration activity	
Location	Noveau Inconnu Lab	
Assumption	Completion of activity by Year 2088	
Constraint	Activity has budget of 200 million USD	

Form 13: Activity Attributes

Milestone List

A milestone list is a list of schedule milestones defining mandatory or optional milestones.

<table>
<tr><td colspan="4" align="center"># Milestone List</td></tr>
<tr><td>**Project Title**</td><td colspan="3">TMX 01</td></tr>
<tr><td colspan="4"></td></tr>
<tr><td>**Project Manager**</td><td>Mary Johnson</td><td>**Date Prepared** | February 13, 2073</td><td>**Last Updated** | February 14, 2073</td></tr>
</table>

Milestone Name	Description	Date
Research Completed	Research will include feasibility of Blue holes, wormholes and cosmic strings phenomena as well as consider time travel methods based on Einstein's famous E=mc2 equation. They will also work on finding a way forward to minimize the requirement of an unthinkably gigantic amount of mass. Other than that the research will prove whether it is possible to cause space time to curve in such a way as to enable travel back in time.	Year 2076
Requirements finalized	Mary Johnson will be responsible to coordinate with everyone in gathering and finalizing requirements. This will include large Hardron Collider or a rocket and technical, natural elements available or possible be built.	Year 2078
Prototype built	After finalization of requirement, the PM together with the Sponsor, customer and specialist will work on building a prototype of the futuristic machine.	Year 2080
Design completed	The design for a device that could be using a ring laser array or Copenhagen/Everrett/Barnes Paradox Solution or other materials compatible at high velocity when relativistic energy and momentum increases	Year 2083
Programing done	Initial plan for the programming is to use JenXc Programing which can be modified thinking of advanced technology after 13 years.	Year 2086
Module Test successful	Whirlpool Affinity Test, Eddies Reverse Reflux Loop Test, Blue hole impact analysis will be used to check and test the machine. Trained animals can be used as sample to test and monitor the effect at earlier stage.	Year 2087
Phase End Review completed	After finalization of requirement, design finalization, and checking of program and functionality, PM will go through review of both modules.	Year 2088

Form 14: TXM01 Milestone List

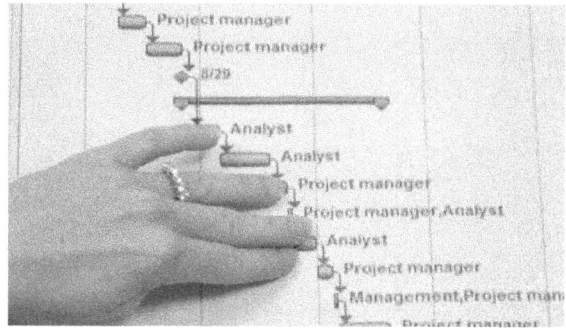

10. Sequence Activities

Once you have defined activities, the next process is Sequence Activities. Activities must be sequenced in the logical order they will occur. The activity list (which is the output of the define activities process) is a major input needed to sequence the activities.

As activities are sequenced, the team should be aware of "dependencies". For example, when building a structure, the foundation must be built first before framing is done. Task A (Build Foundation) precedes Task B (Framing). Task A is the predecessor of Task B. Task B is the successor of Task A.

Inputs	Tools and Techniques	Outputs
● Schedule management plan ● Activity list ● Activity attributes ● Milestone list ● Project scope statement ● Enterprise environmental factors ● Organizational process assets	● Precedence diagramming method (PDM) ● Dependency determination ● Leads and lags	● Project schedule network diagrams ● Project documents updates

Figure 13: Sequence Activities: Inputs, Tools & Techniques and Outputs

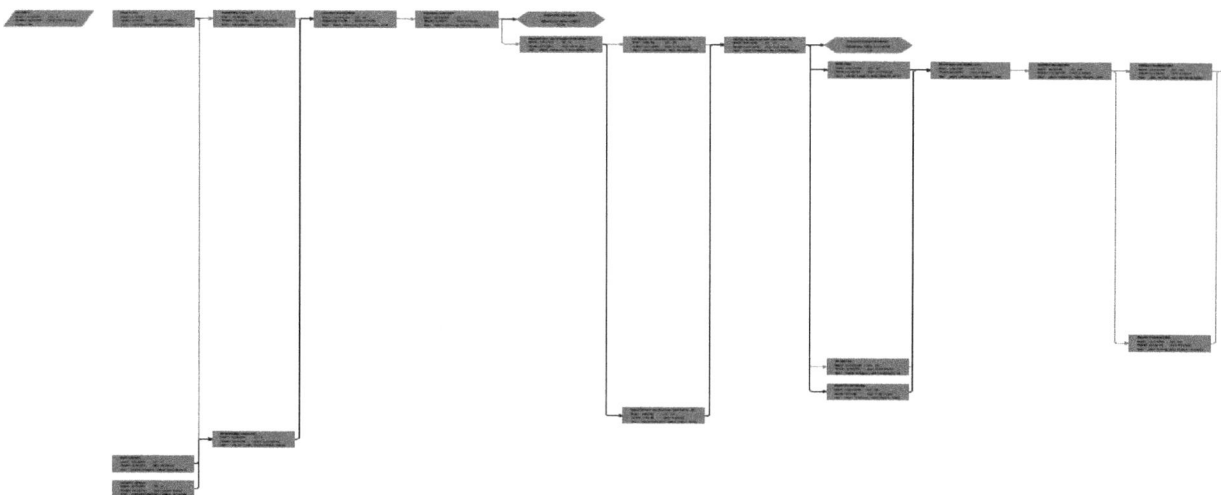

Form 15: TXM01 Schedule Network Diagram

11. Estimate Activity Resources

In this process, the number of resources needed to complete the sequenced activities is estimated. This involves:

- Estimating which resources (human, equipment and material) are needed for the project tasks.

- Knowing when resources will be available to perform the project activities being scheduled.

- The Estimate Activity Resources process is closely associated with the Estimate Costs process in the Project Cost Management Knowledge Area.

Inputs	Tools and Techniques	Outputs
Schedule management plan Activity list Activity attributes Resource calendars Risk register Activity cost estimates Enterprise environmental factors Organizational process assets	Expert judgment Alternative analysis Published estimating data Bottom-up estimating Project management software	Activity resource requirements Resource breakdown structure Project documents updates

Figure 14: Estimate Activity Resources: Inputs, Tools & Techniques and Outputs

Activity Resource Requirements

Identification and description of types and quantities of resources required for schedule activities. This information may be aggregated and used to identify type and quantity of resources needed in each work package.

Activity Resource Requirements

Project Title:		TMX 01				
Project Sponsor:		Alfred Pinkus and Jonny Roberts			Date Prepared:	28-Apr-73
Project Manager:		Mary Johnson			Project Customer:	Professor Zakari

Resource Name	Type	Initials	Max. Units	Std. Rate	Accrue At
Mary Johnson	Work	M	1	$800/hr	Prorated
Bill Brag	Work	B	1	$900/hr	Prorated
Andrew	Work	A	1	$170/hr	Prorated
Henry	Work	H	1	$190/hr	Prorated
Mike	Work	M	1	$800/hr	Prorated
Michael Mathieu	Work	M	1	$750/hr	Prorated
Max Planck	Work	M	1	$700/hr	Prorated
Ney Dimaculangan	Work	N	1	$580/hr	Prorated
Maria Aragon	Work	M	1	$130/hr	Prorated
Alan Turing	Work	A	1	$220/hr	Prorated
Thyro Alfaro	Work	T	1	$350/hr	Prorated
Oh Jin-Hyek	Work	O	1	$600/hr	Prorated
Tirunesh Dibaba	Work	T	1	$500/hr	Prorated
Sally Pearson	Work	S	1	$400/hr	Prorated
Natalya Antyukh	Work	N	1	$380/hr	Prorated
Grinders-MX52.3	Material	G	5	$1,200,000,000	Prorated
Jack-bots300	Material	J	112	$1,690,000,000	Prorated
Krybots5TmXC	Material	K	122	$200,000,000	Prorated
Mecha-Streisand	Material	M	132	$1,445,000,064	Prorated
Mahoro-20H	Material	M	13	$50,000,000	Prorated
Processor Hyper Intelligent Encriptor	Equipment	P	2	$500,000,000	Prorated
Interactive Canine	Equipment	I	14	$299,000,000	Prorated
Robotic Orb	Equipment	r	200	$100,000,000	Prorated
Replicators	Equipment	r	44	$700,000,000	Prorated
Trin-E through Zu-Zana	Equipment	T	22	$398,000,000	Prorated
Weather-controlling robot	Equipment	W	22	$1,800,000,000	Prorated
HMX-17b Milfa_DU	Equipment	H	14	$7,489,999,872	Prorated
HMX-17c Shilfa_DU	Equipment	H	16	$7,489,999,872	Prorated
SILKY(MMF108-41)	Equipment	S	24	$900,000,000	Prorated

Form 16: Activity Resource Requirements

Resource Breakdown Structure

A hierarchical structure of identified resources by category and type. Categories could include: labor, equipment, material and supplies. Resource type could include: skill level and grade level.

```
                            ┌─────────────┐
                            │  RESOURCES  │
                            └──────┬──────┘
        ┌───────────────────────────┼───────────────────────────┐
  ┌───────────┐              ┌───────────┐               ┌───────────┐
  │   Human   │              │ Equipment │               │  Material │
  └─────┬─────┘              └─────┬─────┘               └─────┬─────┘
```

Human
- Resource Name
- Mary Johnson
- Bill Brag
- Andrew
- Henry
- Mike
- Michael Mathieu
- Max Planck
- Ney Dimaculangan
- Maria Aragon
- Alan Turing
- Thyro Alfaro
- Oh Jin-Hyek
- Tirunesh Dibaba
- Sally Pearson

Equipment
- Processor Hyper Intelligent Encriptor
- Interactive Canine
- Robotic Orb
- Replicators
- Trin-E through Zu-Zana
- Weather-controlling robot
- HMX-17b Milfa_DU
- HMX-17c Shilfa_DU
- SILKY(MMF108-41)

Material
- Grinders-MX52.3
- Jack-bots300
- Krybots5TmXC
- Mecha-Streisand
- Mahoro-20H

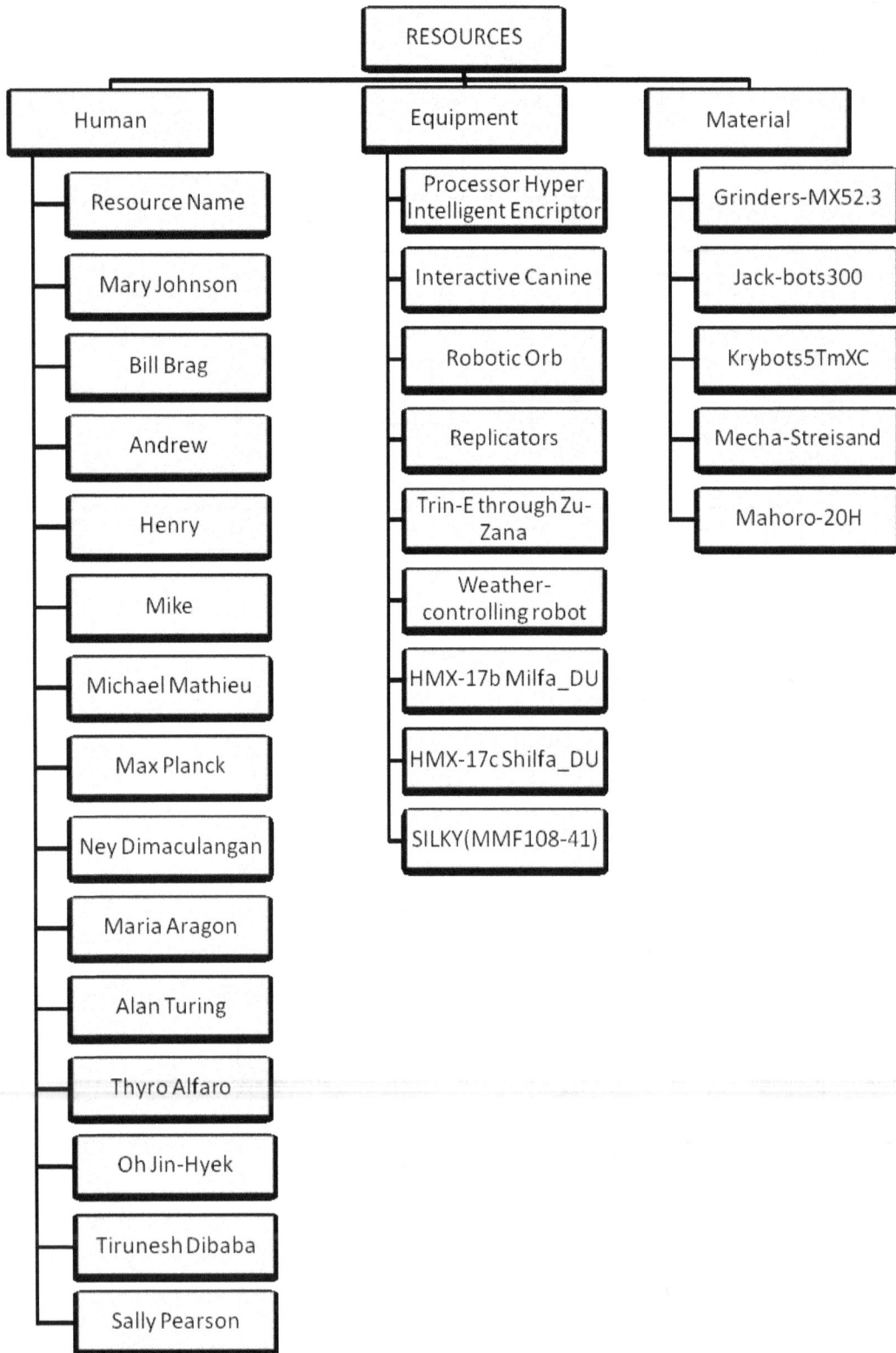

Form 17: Resource Breakdown Structure

12 Estimate Activity Durations

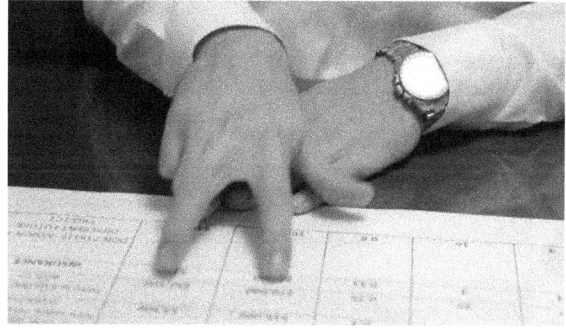

Defining the duration (number of work periods) required for completion of schedule activities. This process:

- Uses information on activity scope of work.
- Considers required resource types, estimated resource quantities, resource calendars, sequencing logic and availability of input data.

Duration estimates may at times be progressively elaborated and the whole duration estimating process is performed by taking into consideration constraints and assumptions.

Inputs	Tools and Techniques	Outputs
• Schedule management plan • Activity list • Activity attributes • Activity resource requirements • Resource calendars • Project scope statement • Risk register • Resource breakdown structure • Enterprise environmental factors • Organizational process assets	• Expert judgment • Analogous estimating • Parametric estimating • Three-point estimating • Group decision-making techniques • Reserve analysis	• Activity duration estimates • Project documents updates

Figure 15: Estimate Activity Durations

Activity Duration Estimates

The duration (number of work periods) required for completion of schedule activities. This may indicate a range of possible results for e.g. 1 month + 7 days, or 75% certain an activity will be completed in a month.

Duration Estimation Worksheet

Project Title	TMX 01

Project Manager	Mary Johnson
Date Prepared	19-Feb-33
Last Updated	20-Feb-33

Analogous Estimate

In 1990 Mallett's focus on his mission of Time Travel invention is intensified with laser-like precision. He devoured every opportunity of Einstein, boned up on differential equations and tensor calculus. By the year 1999, at Penn State, he finally declared his project closure showing that spaces time with two finite parallel cosmic strings each other with sufficient velocity contains closed time like curve. He mentioned that it is impossible to have enough mass in an open universe to build the time machine from the product of decays of stationary particles after long 9 years project work. TMX01 project will be working on similar types with double duration if mentioned obstacles can be

Parametric Estimate

ID	Effort Month Resource	Resource Quantity	% Available	Performance factor	Duration Estimate (Month)
1.1.1	50	3	100	0.6	10.0
1.1.2	40	3	100	0.6	8.0
1.1.3	35	2	100	0.6	10.6
1.2.1	43	3	100	0.7	10.0
1.2.2	20	2	100	0.7	7.2
1.3.1	14	2	100	0.7	5.0
1.3.2	14	2	100	0.7	5.0
2.1.1	25	2	100	0.8	10.0
2.1.2	14	2	100	0.8	5.7
2.2.1	8	2	100	0.8	3.0
2.2.2	2	2	100	0.8	0.7
3.1.1	6	2	100	0.7	2.2
3.1.2	16	3	100	0.7	3.7
3.1.3	4	2	100	0.7	1.4
3.2.1	9	3	100	0.7	2.0
3.2.2	9	3	100	0.7	2.0
3.3.1	9	2	100	0.7	3.0
3.3.2	9	2	100	0.7	3.0
3.4.1	6	2	100	0.7	2.0
3.4.2	6	2	100	0.7	2.0
3.4.3	6	2	100	0.7	2.0
4.1.1	3	2	100	0.8	1.1
4.1.2	4	2	100	0.8	1.7
4.2.1	3	2	100	0.8	1.0
4.2.2	3	2	100	0.8	1.4
4.2.3	5	2	100	0.8	2.0
4.3.1	5	2	100	0.8	2.0
4.3.2	10	2	100	0.8	4.0

Duration Estimation Worksheet

4.4.1	63	4	100	0.8	12.5
4.4.2	11	3	100	0.8	3.0
5.1.1	11	2	100	0.7	3.8
5.1.2	69	3	100	0.7	16.0
5.1.3	25	3	100	0.7	5.8
5.2.1	4	2	100	0.7	1.4
5.2.2	42	3	100	0.7	9.9
5.2.3	8	3	100	0.7	1.8
6.1.1	3	2	100	0.7	1.0
6.1.2	1	2	100	0.7	0.5
6.2.1	4	2	100	0.7	1.5
6.2.2	21	3	100	0.7	5.0
6.2.3	3	2	100	0.7	1.0
7.1.1	11	3	100	0.8	3.0
7.1.2	9	2	100	0.8	3.5
7.1.3	8	3	100	0.8	2.0
7.2.1	11	3	100	0.8	3.0
7.2.2	6	3	100	0.8	1.5
7.2.3	3	2	100	0.8	1.0

Three Point Estimate					
ID	Pessimistic	Most Likely	Optimistic	Weighting Equation	Duration Estimate
1.1.1	12.0	10.0	8	(P+4M+O)/6	10.0
1.1.2	10.0	7.8	7	(P+4M+O)/6	8.0
1.1.3	12.6	10.8	8	(P+4M+O)/6	10.6
1.2.1	12.0	10.0	8	(P+4M+O)/6	10.0
1.2.2	9.2	7.0	6	(P+4M+O)/6	7.2
1.3.1	7.0	4.8	4	(P+4M+O)/6	5.0
1.3.2	7.0	4.8	4	(P+4M+O)/6	5.0
2.1.1	12.0	9.8	9	(P+4M+O)/6	10.0
2.1.2	7.7	5.7	4	(P+4M+O)/6	5.7
2.2.1	5.0	2.6	2.5	(P+4M+O)/6	3.0
2.2.2	2.0	0.4	0.5	(P+4M+O)/6	0.7
3.1.1	3.0	2.1	2	(P+4M+O)/6	2.2
3.1.2	5.5	3.4	3	(P+4M+O)/6	3.7
3.1.3	3.5	0.9	1	(P+4M+O)/6	1.4
3.2.1	4.0	1.6	1.5	(P+4M+O)/6	2.0
3.2.2	4.0	1.6	1.5	(P+4M+O)/6	2.0
3.3.1	5.0	2.8	2	(P+4M+O)/6	3.0
3.3.2	5.0	2.8	2	(P+4M+O)/6	3.0
3.4.1	4.0	1.6	1.5	(P+4M+O)/6	2.0
3.4.2	4.0	1.6	1.5	(P+4M+O)/6	2.0
3.4.3	4.0	1.6	1.5	(P+4M+O)/6	2.0
4.1.1	3.0	0.7	1	(P+4M+O)/6	1.1

Duration Estimation Worksheet

4.1.2	4.0	1.2	1.5	(P+4M+O)/6	1.7
4.2.1	3.0	0.5	1	(P+4M+O)/6	1.0
4.2.2	3.5	0.9	1.2	(P+4M+O)/6	1.4
4.2.3	4.0	1.6	1.5	(P+4M+O)/6	2.0
4.3.1	4.0	1.6	1.5	(P+4M+O)/6	2.0
4.3.2	6.0	3.8	3	(P+4M+O)/6	4.0
4.4.1	14.5	12.1	12	(P+4M+O)/6	12.5
4.4.2	5.0	2.6	2.5	(P+4M+O)/6	3.0
5.1.1	6.0	3.5	3	(P+4M+O)/6	3.8
5.1.2	18.0	16.5	12	(P+4M+O)/6	16.0
5.1.3	8.0	5.4	5	(P+4M+O)/6	5.8
5.2.1	4.0	0.8	1	(P+4M+O)/6	1.4
5.2.2	12.0	9.6	9	(P+4M+O)/6	9.9
5.2.3	4.0	1.5	1	(P+4M+O)/6	1.8
6.1.1	3.0	0.6	0.5	(P+4M+O)/6	1.0
6.1.2	2.5	0.1	0.3	(P+4M+O)/6	0.5
6.2.1	3.5	1.1	1	(P+4M+O)/6	1.5
6.2.2	7.0	4.8	4	(P+4M+O)/6	5.0
6.2.3	3.0	0.6	0.5	(P+4M+O)/6	1.0
7.1.1	5.0	2.8	2	(P+4M+O)/6	3.0
7.1.2	5.5	3.1	3	(P+4M+O)/6	3.5
7.1.3	4.0	1.6	1.5	(P+4M+O)/6	2.0
7.2.1	5.0	2.8	2	(P+4M+O)/6	3.0
7.2.2	3.5	1.1	1	(P+4M+O)/6	1.5
7.2.3	3.0	0.6	0.7	(P+4M+O)/6	1.0

Form 1: Duration Estimation Worksheet

13 Develop Schedule

Developing a realistic and formally approved schedule which is agreed on by the Project Team. The schedule is created by analyzing the sequence of activities, durations, dependencies, schedule constraints and resource requirements.

Developing a project schedule should be based on:

- Analysis of activity sequences
- Activity durations
- Resource requirements
- Schedule constraints

In cases where scheduling software is used, entering activities, durations and resources into the tool may produce a schedule with planned dates that indicate start and finish dates for the activities.

Inputs	Tools and Techniques	Outputs
Schedule management plan Activity list Activity attributes Project schedule network diagrams Activity resource requirements Resource calendars Activity duration estimates Project scope statement Risk register Project staff assignments Resource breakdown structure Enterprise environmental factors Organizational process assets	Schedule network analysis Critical path method Critical chain method Resource optimization techniques Modeling techniques Leads and lags Schedule compression Scheduling tool	Schedule baseline Project schedule Schedule data Project calendars Project management plan updates Project documents updates

Figure 16: Develop Schedule: Inputs, Tools & Techniques and Outputs

Project Schedule

The project schedule includes planned start and planned finish date for each resource activity. It can be represented in graphical or tabular formats.

ID	O	WBS	Task Mode	Task Name	Duration	Start	Finish
0		0		baseline	137.6 mons	2/14/33	12/9/48
1		1.1.1		Blue holes	10 mons	2/14/33	4/7/34
2		1.1.2		Wormholes	8 mons	2/14/33	1/13/34
3		1.1.3		Cosmic strings	10.63 mons	2/14/33	9/22/34
4		1.2.1		Relativity research	10 mons	9/25/34	11/16/35
5		1.2.2		Gravitation research	7.17 mons	9/25/34	10/3/35
6		1.3.1		Conflict Resolution	5 mons	11/19/35	6/13/36
7		1.3.2		Possible outcome	5 mons	6/16/36	1/9/37
8				Research Complete	0 days	1/9/37	1/9/37
9		2.1.1		Mandatory requirement (Module-1)	10 mons	1/12/37	3/5/38
10		2.1.2		Optional requirement (Module-1)	5.73 mons	3/8/38	12/13/38
11		2.2.1		Mandatory requirement (Module-2)	3 mons	3/8/38	7/9/38
12		2.2.2		Optional requirement (Module-2)	0.7 mons	9/21/38	12/13/38
13		0		Requirements finalized	0 days	12/13/38	12/13/38
14		3.1.1		Wiki CAD	2.2 mons	12/14/38	4/18/39
15		3.1.2		6D Mc-do	3.67 mons	12/14/38	5/30/39
16		3.1.3		Rapid Prototyping	1.37 mons	12/14/38	3/7/39
17		3.2.1		Check less expensive way	2 mons	5/31/39	8/22/39
18		3.2.2		Conflict Resolution	2 mons	8/23/39	11/14/39
19		3.3.1		Pattern making plan	3 mons	11/15/39	3/19/40
20		3.3.2		Model making plan	3 mons	11/15/39	3/19/40
21		3.4.1		Crude prototype	2 mons	3/20/40	6/11/40
22		3.4.2		Working prototype	2 mons	6/12/40	9/3/40
23		3.4.3		Final prototype	2 mons	9/4/40	11/26/40
24		0		Prototype builded	0 days	11/26/40	11/26/40
25		4.1.1		Determine inspection goals	1.1 mons	11/27/40	2/15/41
26		4.1.2		Identify features or defects	1.73 mons	10/29/40	2/15/41
27		4.2.1		Material-handling technique	1.03 mons	2/18/41	5/1/41
28		4.2.2		Injection-of-hole (IOH technique)	1.37 mons	2/18/41	6/17/41
29		4.2.3		Any Other	1.97 mons	2/18/41	6/21/41

Project: baseline
Date: 12/15/13

Legend: Task, Split, Milestone, Summary, Project Summary, External Tasks, External Milestone, Inactive Task, Inactive Milestone, Inactive Summary, Manual Task, Duration-only, Manual Summary Rollup, Manual Summary, Start-only, Finish-only, Deadline, Progress

Page 1

Form 18: TMX 01 Project Schedule

14   Plan Cost Management

Plan cost management involves the development of the cost management plan which gives direction on how cost will be managed from start to finish. This process enables project managers to be more intentional about cost management. The key benefit of this process is the guidance and direction the Cost Management Plan gives the team regarding how costs will be managed.

Inputs	Tools and Techniques	Outputs
◦ Project management plan ◦ Project charter ◦ Enterprise environmental factors ◦ Organizational process assets	◦ Expert judgment ◦ Analytical techniques ◦ Meetings	◦ Cost management plan

Figure 17: Plan Cost Management: Inputs, Tools & Techniques and Outputs

Cost Management Plan

Simply put, this is a roadmap for managing cost on the project from project start to end. It contains information that determines how to document, estimate, budget and control project costs. The information contained in the cost management plan is especially helpful to project management teams managing costs on large or high-visibility projects where a lot of structure and order is needed in cost management and reporting based on earned value metrics or other cost management techniques requiring a lot of planning and cost activities.

15 Estimate Costs

The Estimate Costs process involves approximating the monetary resources needed to complete project activities. This involves developing cost approximations for the resources needed for project completion. The estimator should also consider causes of variation including risks.

Cost estimates are expressed in units of currency or other units of measure such as staff hours or days to eliminate the effects of currency fluctuations. Cost estimates should be refined through the course of the project as accuracy of estimates will generally increase as the project progresses. Costs should be estimated for all resources that will be charged to the project.

Inputs	Tools and Techniques	Outputs
Cost management plan Human resource plan Scope baseline Project schedule Risk register Enterprise environmental factors Organizational process assets	Expert judgment Analogous estimating Parametric estimating Bottom-up estimating Three-Point estimates Reserve analysis Cost of quality Project management software Vendor bid analysis Group decision-making techniques	Activity cost estimates Basis of estimates Project documents updates

Figure 18: Estimate Costs: Inputs, Tools & Techniques and Outputs

Activity Cost Estimates

Activity cost estimates is a key output from the Estimate Costs process. Activity cost estimates are assessments of the costs required to complete project activities. This includes direct and indirect costs.

Activity Cost Estimating

Project Title	TMX 01

Project Manager	Mary Johnson
Date Prepared	18-May-33
Last Updated	10-Jun-33

WBS ID	Resource	Direct Costs	Indirect Costs	Reserve	Estimate	Method	Assumption/Constraint	Addt'l Information	Range	Confidence Level
1.1.1	Henry, Mike, Michael Mathieu, Mecha-Streisand	$1,447,010,467	0	0	$1,447,010,467	Parametric	N/A	N/A	(+/-)10%	4
1.1.2	Mike, Ney Dimaculangan, Maria Aragon, Grinders-MX52.3	$1,201,971,200	0	0	$1,201,971,200	Parametric	N/A	N/A	(+/-)10%	5
1.1.3	Mike, Michael Mathieu, Rorschach robote	$802,961,571	0	0	$802,961,571	Analogous	N/A	N/A	(+/-)10%	4
1.2.1	Michael Mathieu, Oh Jin-Hyek, Thyro Alfaro, Jack-bots300	$1,693,072,424	0	0	$1,693,072,424	Parametric	N/A	N/A	(+/-)10%	5
1.2.2	Oh Jin-Hyek, Thyro Alfaro, Galactus Robote	$1,700,994,416	0	0	$1,700,994,416	Parametric	N/A	N/A	(+/-)10%	5
1.3.1	Oh Jin-Hyek, Mary Johnson, Krybots5TmXC	$201,660,805	0	0	$201,660,805	Parametric	N/A	N/A	(+/-)10%	5
1.3.2	Oh Jin-Hyek, Mary Johnson, Lab	$100,679,997	0	0	$100,679,997	Parametric	N/A	N/A	(+/-)10%	6
2.1.1	Mary Johnson, Thyro Alfaro, Trin-E through Zu-Zana	$400,760,012	0	0	$400,760,012	Parametric	N/A	N/A	(+/-)10%	6
2.1.2	Mary Johnson, Ney Dimaculangan, Interactive Canine	$300,489,441	0	0	$300,489,441	Parametric	N/A	N/A	(+/-)10%	5
2.2.1	Mike, Mary Johnson, Trin-E through Zu-Zana	$398,851,194	0	0	$398,851,194	Parametric	N/A	N/A	(+/-)10%	5
2.2.2	Mary Johnson, Ney Dimaculangan, Interactive Canine	$299,140,648	0	0	$299,140,648	Parametric	N/A	N/A	(+/-)10%	6
3.1.1	Max Planck, Maria Aragon, SILKY(MMF108-41)	$900,265,164	0	0	$900,265,164	Parametric	N/A	N/A	(+/-)10%	6
3.1.2	Max Planck, Maria Aragon, Mary Johnson, Mahoro-20H	$50,981,278	0	0	$50,981,278	Parametric	N/A	N/A	(+/-)10%	4
3.1.3	Mary Johnson, Max Planck, Sasquatch switch	$1,100,315,197	0	0	$1,100,315,197	Parametric	N/A	N/A	(+/-)10%	6
3.2.1	Mary Johnson, Max Planck, Ney Dimaculangan, Fin Fang Foom_ModDm	$700,998,369	0	0	$700,998,369	Parametric	N/A	N/A	(+/-)10%	6
3.2.2	Max Planck, Mary Johnson, Lab	$99,719,997	0	0	$99,719,997	Parametric	N/A	N/A	(+/-)10%	6
3.3.1	Max Planck, Ney Dimaculangan, Simulacron-35	$1,000,686,387	0	0	$1,000,686,387	Parametric	N/A	N/A	(+/-)10%	4
3.3.2	Alan Turing, Max Planck, Weather-controlling robot	$1,800,393,523	0	0	$1,800,393,523	Parametric	N/A	N/A	(+/-)10%	5
3.4.1	Alan Turing, Max Planck, Rocket Raccoon_white32	$1,200,441,589	0	0	$1,200,441,589	Parametric	N/A	N/A	(+/-)10%	5
3.4.2	Michael Mathieu, Max Planck, HAL 9000_TC	$2,400,696,074	0	0	$2,400,696,074	Parametric	N/A	N/A	(+/-)10%	6
3.4.3	Max Planck, Mary Johnson, Rorschach robote 2050MX	$220,596,817	0	0	$220,596,817	Parametric	N/A	N/A	(+/-)10%	5
4.1.1	Max Planck, Mike, Interactive Canine	$299,245,608	0	0	$299,245,608	Parametric	N/A	N/A	(+/-)10%	5

Activity Cost Estimating

4.1.2	Max Planck, Mike, replicators	$700,379,217	0	0	$700,379,217	Parametric	N/A	N/A	(+/-)10%	4
4.2.1	Max Planck, Mike, robotic vampire	$100,246,405	0	0	$100,246,405	Parametric	N/A	N/A	(+/-)10%	6
4.2.2	Max Planck, Mike, Müller-Fokker tapes	$200,283,197	0	0	$200,283,197	Parametric	N/A	N/A	(+/-)10%	6
4.2.3	Max Planck, Mike, Reserve for future technology	$300,448,808	0	0	$300,448,808	Parametric	N/A	N/A	(+/-)10%	6
4.3.1	Max Planck, Mary Johnson, Aqua Hunger Force Controller	$500,719,984	0	0	$500,719,984	Parametric	N/A	N/A	(+/-)10%	5
4.3.2	Max Planck, Mary Johnson, Aqua Hunger Force Controller	$501,440,020	0	0	$501,440,020	Parametric	N/A	N/A	(+/-)10%	4
4.4.1	Max Planck, Mary Johnson, Alan Turing, Henry, Titans52Q, Lab, TMT_IN	$505,730,007	0	0	$505,730,007	Parametric	N/A	N/A	(+/-)10%	7
4.4.2	Mary Johnson, Alan Turing, Henry, Lab, TMT_IN	$250,871,193	0	0	$250,871,193	Parametric	N/A	N/A	(+/-)10%	7
5.1.1	Tirunesh Dibaba, Sally Pearson, Processor Hyper Intelligent Encryption	$500,686,397	0	0	$500,686,397	Parametric	N/A	N/A	(+/-)10%	7
5.1.2	Tirunesh Dibaba, Natalya Antyukh, Andrew, HMX-17b Milfa_DU	$7,492,992,368	0	0	$7,492,992,368	Parametric	N/A	N/A	(+/-)10%	6
5.1.3	Tirunesh Dibaba, Natalya Antyukh, Andrew, Simulacron-35	$1,001,213,296	0	0	$1,001,213,296	Parametric	N/A	N/A	(+/-)10%	5
5.2.1	Tirunesh Dibaba, Sally Pearson, Processor Hyper Intelligent Encryption	$500,156,784	0	0	$500,156,784	Parametric	N/A	N/A	(+/-)10%	5
5.2.2	Tirunesh Dibaba, Sally Pearson, Natalya Antyukh, HMX-17c Shilfa_DU	$7,491,947,069	0	0	$7,491,947,069	Parametric	N/A	N/A	(+/-)10%	5
5.2.3	Tirunesh Dibaba, , Natalya Antyukh, Andrew, Simulacron-35	$1,000,262,860	0	0	$1,000,262,860	Parametric	N/A	N/A	(+/-)10%	5
6.1.1	Maria Aragon,Oh Jin-Hyek, Lab	$99,175,198	0	0	$99,175,198	Parametric	N/A	N/A	(+/-)10%	5
6.1.2	Oh Jin-Hyek, Mary Johnson, Processor Hyper Intelligent Encryption	$500,168,007	0	0	$500,168,007	Parametric	N/A	N/A	(+/-)10%	5
6.2.1	Oh Jin-Hyek, Mary Johnson, Lab, tester	$148,504,002	0	0	$148,504,002	Parametric	N/A	N/A	(+/-)10%	7
6.2.2	Oh Jin-Hyek, Mary Johnson, Maria Aragon, Lab, Simulacron-35, CCO	$3,768,836,096	0	0	$3,768,836,096	Parametric	N/A	N/A	(+/-)10%	7
6.2.3	Oh Jin-Hyek, Mary Johnson, Interactive Canine, Lab	$398,336,000	0	0	$398,336,000	Parametric	N/A	N/A	(+/-)10%	5
7.1.1	Henry, Ney Dimaculangan, Mike, TMTX2050 robote	$199,068,078	0	0	$199,068,078	Parametric	N/A	N/A	(+/-)10%	6
7.1.2	Ney Dimaculangan, Mike, Lab, Tester	$149,038,561	0	0	$149,038,561	Parametric	Can be increased	N/A	(+/-)15%	6
7.1.3	Mike, Bill Brag, Henry, Lab	$99,813,601	0	0	$99,813,601	Parametric	N/A	N/A	(+/-)10%	6
7.2.1	Bill Brag, Henry, Mary Johnson, TMTX2050 robote	$199,286,312	0	0	$199,286,312	Parametric	N/A	N/A	(+/-)10%	6
7.2.2	Bill Brag, Ney Dimaculangan, Mary Johnson, Lab, tester	$148,728,002	0	0	$148,728,002	Parametric	N/A	N/A	(+/-)10%	6
7.2.3	Mary Johnson, Bill Brag, Lab	$99,285,596	0	0	$99,285,596	Parametric	N/A	N/A	(+/-)10%	5

Form 19: Activity Cost Estimates

Determine Budget

Determine Budget involves aggregating or collectively summing up the costs of estimated schedule activities or work packages to establish a total cost performance baseline for managing project performance.

Inputs	Tools and Techniques	Outputs
● Cost management plan ● Scope baseline ● Activity cost estimates ● Basis of estimates ● Project schedule ● Resource calendars ● Risk register ● Agreements ● Organizational process assets	● Cost aggregation ● Reserve analysis ● Expert judgment ● Historical relationships ● Funding limit reconciliation	● Cost baseline ● Project funding requirements ● Project documents updates

Figure 19: Determine Budget: Inputs, Tools & Techniques and Outputs

Cost Performance Baseline

The Cost Performance Baseline is the authorized budget at completion (BAC) that is used to measure and control project cost performance.

Cost Budget

Project Title		TMX 01
Project Manager		Mary Johnson
Date Prepared		18-May-33
Last Updated		10-Jun-33

WBS ID	Project Phase	Phase Budget
1.0	PHASE 1	$7,148,350,800
2.0	PHASE 2	$1,399,241,280
3.0	PHASE 3	$9,475,094,498
4.0	PHASE 4	$3,359,364,400
5.0	PHASE 5	$17,987,259,360
6.0	PHASE 6	$4,915,019,200
7.0	PHASE 7	$10,842,404,960
TOTAL		**$55,126,734,498**

Form 20: TMX 01 Budget

17 | Plan Quality Management

Plan Quality Management involves identifying quality requirements and standards that are relevant to the project or product and how to satisfy them. Plan Quality should be performed in parallel with other project planning processes. Inputs from project scope, cost, time and risk areas are key inputs when planning quality as well as defining Perform Quality Assurance and Control Quality activities.

Inputs	Tools and Techniques	Outputs
<ul><li>Project management plan</li><li>Stakeholder register</li><li>Risk register</li><li>Requirements documentation</li><li>Enterprise environmental factors</li><li>Organizational process assets</li></ul>	<ul><li>Cost-benefit analysis</li><li>Cost of quality</li><li>Seven basic quality tools</li><li>Benchmarking</li><li>Design of experiments</li><li>Statistical sampling</li><li>Additional quality planning tools</li><li>Meetings</li></ul>	<ul><li>Quality management plan</li><li>Process improvement plan</li><li>Quality metrics</li><li>Quality checklists</li><li>Project documents updates</li></ul>

Figure 20: Plan Quality Management: Inputs, Tools & Techniques and Outputs

Quality can be defined as fitness for use or conformance to requirements. In cases where it is not properly defined, quality could be perceptual, conditional and subjective.

A customer may define quality of a product or service as how it compares to competitors in the marketplace. Production organizations may define quality in terms of the level of conformance to a set of data requirements to which the product was produced.

Quality Management Plan

The Quality Management Plan describes project quality standards, quality policies & procedures of an organization and how a project team will implement and assess effectiveness of the quality assurance and quality control processes on a project.

Quality Management plan				
Project Title:	TMX 01			
Project Sponsor:	Alfred Pinkus and Jonny Roberts		**Date Prepared:**	11-Mar-33
Project Manager:	Mary Johnson		**Project Customer:**	Professor Zakari

Introduction

Quality management plan for the TMX 01 project will create the processes as well as activities to ensure a quality product. The goal is to ensure quality is well planned, appropriately defined how it will be managed, define quality assurance activities & quality control activities and as well as acceptable limit of quality standards.

Quality management approaches

Product quality for TMX 01 will be defined by the Noveau Inconnu's standards and criteria for Professor Zakari. The main concern is on the deliverables, standards and criteria used will ensure the product meets established quality standards and customer satisfaction. On the other hand process quality for the project will work on the processes by which the project deliverable will be mass-produced. Establishing process quality standards will ensure that all activities conform to Noveau Inconnu standard which results to success.

Quality metrics will be used to measure quality throughout the project life cycle for the product and processes. Mary Johnson will be responsible for working with the project team to define these metrics, conduct measurements, and analyze results.

Quality standards and requirements

Product quality

The product quality standards will be based on the Noveau Inconnu's documented standards for TMX 01 projects. A quality team can be formed lead by Mary Johnson will review if any newly identified standards requirement later and incorporate them into organizational documentation if approved by management.

Process quality

The process quality standards will be based on the Noveau Inconnu's documented standards for the projects. A quality team can be formed lead by Mary Johnson will review if any newly identified standards requirement later and incorporate them into organizational documentation if approved by management. The updated process quality will be communicated to all stakeholders involved in the project.

Quality roles and responsibilities

Roles	Responsibilities
Work on research with standard quality	Mary Johnson
Requirement finalization under quality guideline	Mary Johnson
Building of prototype with expected quality	Mary Johnson
Completion of design with desired quality	Mary Johnson
Working on programming with standard quality	Mary Johnson
Testing modules with quality standard	Mary Johnson
Phase end review with quality standard	Mary Johnson

Quality Assurance

Mary Johnson and other team members will perform assessments at planned intervals to ensure all processes are being correctly implemented and executed all the way. Mary Johnson will provide quality management daily and conduct process audits on at least weekly basis, monitor process performance metrics. If discrepancies are found, she will work with sponsor with the identified discrepancies.

Quality Management plan

				Quality Assurance Record			
Trial Number	Date of trial	Process Measured	Expected Value	Actual Measured	Accepta ble (Y/N)	Recommendation	Resolved (Y/N)
1	8-Mar-37	Work on research with standard quality	Begin with determining what are the areas need to research and which are the machine and measuring tools need to be available at Lab.	A team member stated that one of the scientist in Germany built blue holes at our desired outcome. So it is possible to outsource the material.	N	Change process as to search latest/ modern update of the research and contact with them before start of work for the specific research area.	Y
2	17-Mar-38	Requirement finalization under quality guideline	Begin with determining which product and equipment are required to build time machine and make a list of that with cost comparison	With the list of mandatory requirement, two of the optional requirement are actually build-in at FOX-366 device that would reduce cost for both the modules.	N	After list need to analyze and identify non required requirements before purchase and cost estimate.	Y

Quality Control
Mary Johnson will schedule regularly occurring project, management, and document reviews. She will review products as well as any discrepancies and audit findings and also discussion on product improvement initiatives. The primary measurement will be conducted by respective team members and any discrepancies will be solved through Mary Johnson.

				Quality Control Record			
Trial Number	Date of trial	Process Measured	Expected Value	Actual Measured	Accepta ble (Y/N)	Recommendation	Resolved (Y/N)
1	30-Jul-13	Testing modules with quality standard	While working with crude prototype FTT measurements should be measured in KALVO (%K) scale and will need to be limited by 0.001 s mili cycle.	Crude prototype is measured for FTT measurements is measured in KALVO (%K) scale but limited by 0.01 s mili cycle.	N	Replace scale with 0.001 s scale	Y
2	3-Aug-47	Phase end review with quality standard	Phase end review should follow the ten steps of quality standard of Sigma-1045	Project follows the ten steps of quality standard of Sigma-1045	Y	No	Y

Approvals			
Project Manager Signature		Sponsor or Originator Signature	
Project Manager Name		Sponsor or Originator Name	
Date		Date	

Form 21: Quality Management Plan

Process Improvement Plan

A process improvement plan identifies the current processes and their complexities, analyzes the processes, measures actual performance against standards, and develops a plan for improvement. It describes steps for continuous monitoring of processes to identify poor quality and develop ways to enhance future performance.

Process Improvement plan

Project Title:		TMX 01	

Project Sponsor:	Alfred Pinkus and Jonny Roberts	Date Prepared:	23-Jun-33
Project Manager:	Mary Johnson	Project Customer:	Professor Zakari

Purpose

The plan will establish criteria for development of TMX01 project that Noveau Inconnu is working on. The process improvement plan will describe the implementation management processes and analyze it to continually monitor and improve. This plan will be followed throughout the project's life cycle and will lay out the steps to identify, measure and implement the process to improve.

Process Description

TMX01 project will work on the established process stored in organizational process asset. Mary Johnson will be the project manager as well as key person to make the project successful. Any process improvement will be raised by Mary Johnson and will be implemented once approved. The main goal of the plan is to setup an acceptable criteria for event organizing for the future project.

Process Matrix

?	Gather & Organize data
?	Review Present performance
?	Describe significant trends
?	Perform challenging prioritization

?	Go for root cause analysis
?	Find improvement strategies
?	Find benchmark

?	Set up performance target
?	Find Interim Measure

Targets for Improvement

It would be great if TMX01 project potentially result to significant savings of cost and time. It would be a risk because there is no previous project done similar to this one.

Criteria	Current	Target
Cost saving	Present Project	Cost effective than estimated
Time saving	Present Project	Time effective than estimated
Quality	Present Project	High quality than estimated

Process Improvement Approach

TMX01 project is committed to continuous improvement across its projects and project teams. The plan describes a formal key performance indicator evaluation process that will further facilitate continuous improvement. The KPI process is a whole life project process of evaluating key performance indicators and team key performance indicators. Any KPI used within the project process needs to be consistent, realistic measureable, unequivocal, auditable, and of value as well as should inform the reviewer, enabling action to be

Approvals

Project Manager Signature		Sponsor or Originator Signature	

Project Manager Name		Sponsor or Originator Name	
Date		Date	

Form 22: Process Improvement Plan

PRAIZION MEDIA

18 Plan Human Resource Management

The Plan Human Resource Management process involves identifying and documenting Project Team roles, responsibilities and reporting relationships. The output of this process is the Human Resource Plan. Clarifying roles and responsibilities is very important when managing a team. Responsibilities of the Project Manager in this process may include:

- Attending meetings
- Identifying training needs
- Team building strategies
- Plans for recognition and rewards
- Safety issues

Inputs	Tools and Techniques	Outputs
• Project management plan • Activity resource requirements • Enterprise environmental factors • Organizational process assets	• Organization charts and position descriptions • Networking • Organizational theory • Expert judgment • Meetings	• Human resource management plan

Figure 21: Plan Human Resource Management: Inputs, Tools & Techniques and Outputs

Human Resource Plan

The Human Resource Plan consists of guidelines on how project human resources will be defined, staffed, monitored, controlled and released. It includes project assignments, roles and responsibilities, organizational charts, staffing management plans, recognition and reward programs, training needs and team building strategies. This document could contain a lot of information and needs to be understood.

Human Resource Management Plan

Project Title:		TMX 01		
Project Sponsor:	Alfred Pinkus and Jonny Roberts		**Date Prepared:**	25-Feb-73
Project Manager:	Mary Johnson		**Project Customer:**	Professor Zakari

Introduction

The plan will be used as a tool to aid in the management of TMX 01 project's human resource activities throughout the project until finished. It includes roles and responsibilities of team members, project organization charts and staffing management plan.

Roles and responsibilities

Name	Role	Authority	Responsibility	Competency
Mary Johnson	PM	Mary Johnson has the authority to acquire human resources for the project through coordination with other managers, authorize and approve all project expenditures as well as reviewing the activities that meet established acceptability criteria.	Responsible for the overall project success. Mary Johnson will also be responsible for reporting the project status in accordance with the communication management plan and will evaluate the performance of team members and forwarding their performance to other managers and sponsor.	Effective communication, leadership, management, budgeting, scheduling
Mike	Mid level Manager	Mike has the authority to coordinate all electronics issues at research phase.	Responsible for the research phase of the project. He will be also responsible for reporting research status in accordance with the communication management plan and will evaluate the performance of team members and communicate their performance to PM.	Effective Researcher and good communication
Bill Brag	Program manager	Bill Brag has the authority to audit and investigate overall project status as well as provide project prioritization	Supervision & prioritizes the project	Strategic Thinking, External Awareness, Entrepreneurship
Maria Aragon	Accounts manager	Work on costing control at all activity	Responsible for internal financial analysis and monitoring of budget and forecast constraints as well as procurement and cost control	Financial analysis, procurement
Alan Turing	Team member	Work for socio-cognitive linguistics	Ensure communication throughout the project	Effective communication
Thyro Alfaro	Fluid specialist	Support on fluid dynamics at research phase	Successful completion of research phase	Effective Researcher
Oh Jin-Hyek	Relativity tester	Work as relativity certified administrator	Successful completion of research and design phase	Effective Researcher, administrator and supporter
Tirunesh Dibaba	JenXc Programmer	Provide programming support in the programming phase	Successful completion of programming stage	Effective technical skill
Sally Pearson	Team member	Provide programming support in the programming phase	Successful completion of programming stage	Effective technical skill
Natalya Antyukh	Team member	Provide design support in the design phase	Design support in the design phase	Effective technical skill
Ney Dimaculangan	Team member	Dynamic field research in the research phase	Successful completion of the research phase	Effective Researcher
Andrew	Team member	Socio-cognitive Linguistics	Ensure communication throughout the project	Linguistics, effective communication
Henry	Team member	Ensure safety and provide tactical advice at all activity	Successful completion of safety issue in terms of data, machine as well as overall project	Safety guideline
Michael Mathieu	Adaptive mesh refinement specialist	Support in the research phase	Successful completion of research phase	Effective Researcher
Max Planck	Design support	Support in the design phase	Successful completion of design phase	Effective technical skill

Human Resource Management Plan

Project organizational charts

Role	PM	Planner and developer	Tester	Admin assistant
Blue holes	A	R	C	
Wormholes	A	R	C	
Cosmic strings	A	R	C	
Relativity research	A	R	C	
Gravitation research	A	R	C	
Conflict Resolution	R	C		R
Possible outcome	A	R	C	R
Mandatory requirement (Module- 1)	R	C	I	I
Optional requirement (Module- 1)	R	C	I	I
Mandatory requirement (Module- 2)	R	C	I	I
Optional requirement (Module- 2)	R	C	I	I
WiKi CAD	A	R	R	
6D Mic-do	A	R	R	
Rapid Prototyping	A	R	R	
Check less expensive way	A	R	I	R
Conflict Resolution	R	C	C	R
Pattern making plan	A	R	C	
Model making plan	A	R	C	
Crude prototype	A	R	C	
Working prototype	A	R	C	
Final prototype	A	R	C	I
Determine inspection goals	R	C	C	R
Identify features or defects	I	R	R	I
Material-handling technique	A	R	R	
Injection-of-hole (IOH)	A	R	R	
Any Other	A	R	R	
Integrate motion control	A	R	R	
Interactive development session	A	R	R	
Develop an interface	A	R	R	
Combine	A	R	R	
JenXc program plan (module-1)	A	R	R	I
Execution of programing (module-	A	R	R	
Testing (module-1)	A	R	R	
JenXc program plan (module-2)	A	R	R	I
Execution of programing (module-	A	R	R	
Testing (module-2)	A	R	R	
Preparation	A	R	R	I
Test Steps	A	R	R	
Obtain test result	A	R	R	
Work with deviations	A	R	R	
Prepare final outcome	R	R	I	A
Core values of peer review	A	R	R	
Short out limitations	R	R		
Work with Advisory Council	I	R	R	
Core values of peer review	A	R	R	
Short out limitations	R	R		
Work with Advisory Council	I	R	R	

Staffing management plan

Staff Acquisition

Staff will consist of both internal and external resources for the TMX 01 project. There will be outsourcing and contracting performed within the scope of this project. Mary Johnson will negotiate with other managers and program mangers in identifying and assigning resources as per the project organizational structure. All resources must be approved by the appropriate authority.

Resource Calendars

Resource calendar will be maintained through out the project. Mary Johnson will do any necessary changes as required. Calendar will be attached in the MS project Document sheet

Performance Review

Mary Johnson will review team member's assigned activities at the onset of the project and communicate expectations of work to be performed. She will then evaluate each team member throughout the project to evaluate their performance and how effectively they are completing their assigned work. Prior to releasing project resources, Mary Johnson will provide feedback on employee project performance. Bill Brag will perform a formal performance review on each team member.

Recognition

There will be a party to celebrate the success of each team member with the team member's families present. Alfred Pinkus and Jonny Roberts will issue certificate of appreciation to each team members who satisfactorily completed all assigned work on time.

Human Resource Management Plan

Project and Product Requirements

The project will meet requirement after time travel machine as well as solve the criminal handling problem either by deported back in time or forwarded in future. It's fundamental requirement includes:

-Research of Albert Einstein's theory of special relativity, Mac John classic theory of relative motion
-Huge disk space depends on the initial amount of data that needs to be backed up and how much data changes on an hourly basis
-A extra high speed switching capable machine compatible with the velocity of light
-Measurements of various quantities that are relative to the velocities of observers
-Design that is compatible at high velocity when relativistic energy and momentum increases
-JenXc Programing of the machine
-Whirlpool Affinity Test, Eddies Reverse Reflux Loop Test, Black hole impact analysis

Project Acceptance Criteria

The success of the project will be determined by below mentioned criteria

-Initial plan reviews and agreed by stakeholders involved.
-Expected result delivered to the end user.
-Project implementation with desired budget, time frame and quality as per time, cost and quality management plan to be established later.

Initial and high level Risks

Project cancellation without any outcome: Impact: high, Probability: Medium

-data loss by virtue of no backup: Impact: high, Probability: medium

-side-effect of cloning: Impact: high, Probability: medium

-Natural influence: Impact: high, Probability: low

-Budget limit exceed due to variation of other constraint: Impact: high, Probability: high

-Schedule does not meet the deadline: Impact: medium, Probability: low

Project Objectives	Success Criteria	Person Approving
Scope		
Scope includes all the works and only the works required to transport man wholly and bodily through time. There will be two modules i.e. Forward time travel and Backward time travel modules that will provide the option to transport back in time or forward in future.	Meeting mentioned scope	Sponsor & Customer
Time		
Time duration for the project is 15 years, from 12 February 2073.	Meeting mentioned deadline	Sponsor
Cost		
The initial Budget for the project is $55 Billion Dollars.	Meeting mentioned budget	Sponsor
Quality		
The machine must meet the quality standard from ISTTO and environmental standard from IETO.	Meeting the mentioned quality standard	Sponsor
Other		
Security of the research, design, programming will be maintained strictly as mentioned in security guideline	Meeting the mentioned service	Sponsor & Customer

Key Stakeholders

Name	Role	Responsibility
Alfred Pinkus and Jonny Roberts	Sponsor	Financial support
Professor Zakari	Customer	Supporter
Noveau Inconnu	Organizer	Organizational support
Mary Johnson	PM	Manage the project
Bill Brag	Program manager	Overview and support the project
Andrew	Programmer and contributor to meetings	Programming
Henry	Safety and Tactical advisor	Supervisor and supporter of safety issues
Mike	Mid-level manager	Coordinate all electronic issues

Form **23: Human Resource Management Plan**

19 Plan Communications Management

The Plan Communications Management process involves determining and planning communication requirements, information requirements and procedures on a project. Who sends information to whom, why and when? Effective communication involves communicating in the right format, on time with the right impact. Improper communication will lead to problems such as delay in message delivery, communicating to the wrong audience or lack of communication to stakeholders who need the information. Plan Communications Management also entails analyzing communication channels, communication needs and alternate ways of communicating effectively on the project. Communication planning may be done early but should be regularly revised to accommodate project changes and ensure practicability.

Inputs	Tools and Techniques	Outputs
• Project management plan • Stakeholder register • Enterprise environmental factors • Organizational process assets	• Communication requirements analysis • Communication technology • Communication models • Communication methods • Meetings	• Communications management plan • Project documents updates

Figure 22: Plan Communications Management: Inputs, Tools & Techniques and Outputs

Communications Management Plan

The Communications Management Plan defines the communication needs and expectations of project stakeholders. It describes the format, location and party responsible for the communication. The Communications Management Plan is contained in or is a subsidiary plan of the Project Management Plan.

Communication Management plan

Project Title:		TMX 01	

Project Sponsor:	Alfred Pinkus and Jonny Roberts	Date Prepared:	12-Apr-33
Project Manager:	Mary Johnson	Project Customer:	Professor Zakari

Project Purpose or Business case

The objective of this plan is to identify all communication needs of the project "TMX 01" stakeholders and to ensure the project team is able to carry out a coordinated effort to meet the stakeholders' varied communication needs. This plan will serve as a catalyst for successful project completion by facilitating the information flow required for timely decision-making, action item tracking, status updates, and overall understanding of the project goals and deliverables.

Project Stakeholders

Internal Stakeholders

Name	Role	Responsibility	Contact
Mary Johnson	PM	All the activity	Mary Johnson@email.com
Andrew	Team member	Programmer and contributor to meetings	Andrew@email.com
Henry	Team member	Safety and Tactical advisor	Henry@email.com
Mike	Mid-level manager	coordinator for electronics.	Mike@email.com
Michael Mathieu	Adaptive mesh refinement specialist	Support	Michael Mathieu@email.com
Max Planck	Cosmologic designer	Design support	Max Planck@email.com
Ney Dimaculangan	Team member	Dynamic field researcher	Ney Dimaculangan@email.com
Maria Aragon	Accounts manager	Cost control activity	Maria Aragon@email.com
Alan Turing	Team member	Socio-cognitive Linguistics	Alan Turing@email.com
Thyro Alfaro	Fluid specialist	support on fluid dynamics	Thyro Alfaro@email.com
Oh Jin-Hyek	Relativity tester	Relativity Certified Administrator	Oh Jin-Hyek@email.com
Tirunesh Dibaba	JenXc Programmer	Programming support	Tirunesh Dibaba@email.com
Sally Pearson	Team member	Programming support	Sally Pearson@email.com
Natalya Antyukh	Team member	Design support	Natalya Antyukh@email.com

External Stakeholders

Name	Role	Responsibility	Contact
Alfred Pinkus and Jonny Roberts	Sponsor	Financial support	Alfred Pinkus and Jonny Roberts@email.com
Professor Zakari	Customer	Support	Professor Zakari@email.com
Bill Brag	Program manager	Overview and support project	Bill Brag@email.com

Communication Management plan

Information Collection and Reporting

Requirement	Provider	Collection Frequency	Collection Method	Report/Document Title
Project charters and plans	Alfred Pinkus and Jonny Roberts	Once, when created	Formal documented	Project charter
Communicating with Upper Management and Customers	Mary Johnson	Monthly	E mail memo	Status report
Change Management	Mary Johnson	Monthly	E mail memo, meeting when required	Issue log
Administrative Close-Out	Mary Johnson	When required	Formal documented, meeting when required	Project Approvals
Project closure	Mary Johnson	Once, at the end	Formal documented	Project Close-Out

Information Distribution, Storage and Disposition

Report/Document Title	Target Audience	Primary Notification/ Distribution Method	Secondary Notification/ Distribution Method	Storage/Disposition
Project charter	All	Mary Johnson	Team member	Project Documents
Status report	Alfred Pinkus and Jonny Roberts and Bill Brag	Mary Johnson	Professor Zakari	Project documents
Change Management	Alfred Pinkus and Jonny Roberts	Mary Johnson	Professor Zakari	Project documents
Project Close-Out	Alfred Pinkus and Jonny Roberts and Bill Brag	Mary Johnson	Professor Zakari	Project documents

The Communications Management Plan provides the following:

- *Communications requirements of stakeholders*
- *Intended information format and method*

Content, frequency, responsibility, escalation process, glossary of common terminology, information flowcharts, level of communication, templates for status meetings and guidelines on use of technologies

Communication Management plan

It is imperative that any disputes, conflicts, or discrepancies regarding TMX 01 project communications are resolved in a way that is conducive to maintaining the project schedule, ensuring the correct communications are distributed, and preventing any ongoing difficulties. In order to ensure projects stay on schedule and issues are resolved, company will use its standard escalation model to provide a framework for escalating communication issues. The table below defines the priority levels, decision authorities, and timeframes for resolution.

Priority	Definition	Decision Authority	Timeframe for Resolution
1	Major impact to project or business operations. If not resolved quickly there will be a significant adverse impact to revenue and/or schedule.	Professor Zakari	Within 2 business day
2	Medium impact to project or business operations which may result in some adverse impact to revenue and/or schedule.	Professor Zakari	Within one business week
3	Slight impact which may cause some minor scheduling difficulties with the project but no impact to business operations or revenue.	Mary Johnson	Within two business week
4	Insignificant impact to project but there may be a better solution.	Mary Johnson	Work continues and any recommendations are submitted via the project change control process

Approvals

Project Manager Signature		Sponsor or Originator Signature	
Project Manager Name		Sponsor or Originator Name	
Date		Date	

Form 24: Communication Management Plan

20   Plan Risk Management

The ultimate goal of the Plan Risk Management process is to develop the Risk Management Plan which defines how risks will be identified, evaluated and managed on the project.

All intended processes for conducting risk management should be defined in detail to a degree suitable for the project and comparable to the cost, size and importance of the project to the organization. Success of all other processes of project risk management depends largely on how well the Plan Risk Management Plan process was performed.

Inputs	Tools and Techniques	Outputs
◉ Project management plan ◉ Project charter ◉ Stakeholder register ◉ Enterprise environmental factors ◉ Organizational process assets	◉ Analytical techniques ◉ Expert judgment ◉ Meetings	◉ Risk management plan

Figure 23: Plan Risk Management: Inputs, Tools & Techniques and Outputs

Risk Management Plan

The Risk Management Plan defines and documents how project risks will be identified, analyzed, monitored, controlled and managed. The Risk Management Plan is essentially a document that explains how risk management activities will be performed throughout the project. It also may contain information regarding:

- Risk management methodology.

- Roles and Responsibilities.

- Risk probability and impact.

- Budgeting: resource assignment and fund estimates for risk management should be included in the cost performance baseline.

- Timing: frequency for performing risk management processes through the project life-cycle.

- Protocols for application of schedule contingency reserves and risk management activities for inclusion in the project schedule.

- Risk categories: defining a structure for systematically identifying risks to a consistent level of detail. The Risk Breakdown Structure (RBS) may be developed at this stage. The Risk Management Plan should contribute to the Identify Risks process. This can be achieved using a Risk Breakdown Structure (RBS) which lists the categories and subcategories within which risks may arise on a project.

- A Risk Breakdown Structure (RBS) is a hierarchical break down of project risks according to risk category and sub-category. It is used to identify areas and causes of potential risk.

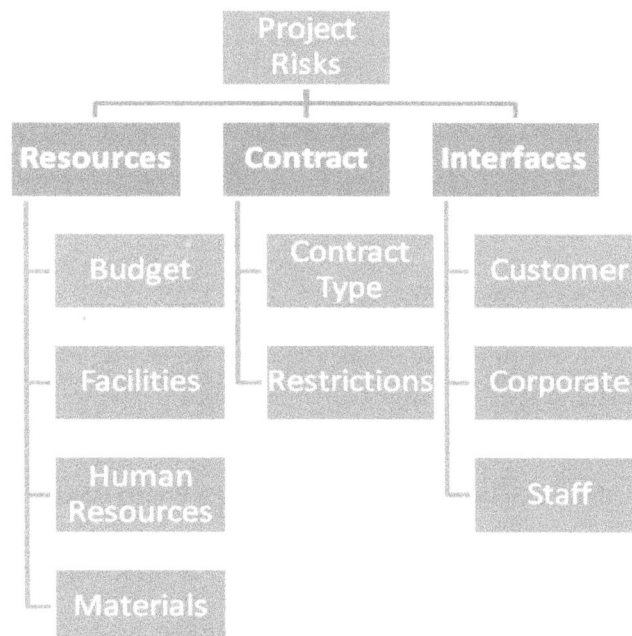

Figure 24: Risk Breakdown Structure

- Revised stakeholder tolerances: stakeholder tolerances applying to the project may be revised in plan risk management.

- Reporting formats: defining how to document, analyze and report outcomes of risk management processes. Describing content and format of the Risk Register and other required risk reports.

- Tracking: defining how to record or track risk activities on the project and how risk management processes will be audited.

- Definitions of risk probability and impact: definitions of probability levels and impacts are suited to the project for use in the Perform Qualitative Risk Analysis process. Included in this plan may be examples of definitions of negative impacts that could be used in evaluating risk impacts related to four project objectives of time, cost, scope and quality.

Defined Conditions for Impact Scales of Risk on Project Objectives					
Project Objective	Relative or numerical scales				
	Very low / 5%	Low/10%	Moderate / 20%	High /40%	Very high / 80%
Cost	Insignificant cost increase	< 10% cost increase	10-20% cost increase	20-40% cost increase	>40% cost increase
Time	Insignificant time increase	< 5% time increase	5-10% time increase	10-20% time increase	>20% time increase
Scope	Scope decrease barely noticeable	Minor areas of scope affected	Major areas of scope affected	Scope reduction unacceptable to sponsor	Project end item is effectively useless
Quality	Quality degradation barely noticeable	Only very demanding applications are affected	Quality reduction requires sponsor approval	Quality reduction unacceptable to sponsor	Project end item is effectively useless
Performance	Minimal consequence to objectives/goals	Minor consequence to objectives/goals	Unable to achieve a particular objective/ goal, but remaining objective goals represent better than minimum success or outcome	Unable to achieve multiple objectives/goals but minimum success can still be achieved or claimed	Unable to achieve objectives/goals such that minimum success cannot be achieved or claimed
Safety/ Human	Discomfort or nuisance	First aid event per OSHA criteria	No lost time injury or illness per OSHA criteria	No lost time injury or illness per OSHA criteria	Loss of life
Asset	Minimal consequence: asset has no sign of physical damage	Minor consequence: asset has cosmetic damage and is repairable	Minor consequence: asset is damaged but repairable	Major consequence asset is substantially damaged but repairable	Destroyed: asset is compromised, and un-repairable: a total loss

Figure 25: Definition of Impact Scales for Project Objectives

- Probability and Impact Matrix: this is a look-up table documenting combinations of probability of a risk occurring and its likely impact or rating in descriptive terms (for example low, medium or high) or numbers 0 – 100. It could also contain specific combinations of probability and impact that contribute to a risk being categorized as high, moderate or low importance.

These values or descriptions can further be color coded or highlighted to give a quick high-level assessment of project risks. It also gives an idea of the kind of effort required to manage risks.

PROBABILITY (scale of 0 - 1)		Very low / 0.05	Low 0.10	Moderate 0.20	High 0.40	Very high 0.80
Almost Certain	0.90	0.05	0.09	0.18	0.36	0.72
Highly Likely	0.70	0.04	0.07	0.14	0.28	0.56
Likely	0.50	0.03	0.05	0.10	0.20	0.40
Low Likelyhood	0.30	0.02	0.03	0.06	0.12	0.24
Not Likely	0.10	0.01	0.01	0.02	0.04	0.08

THREATS IMPACT (SCALE 0 - 1)

Form 25: Probability – Impact Matrix

Risk Management plan

Project Title:		TMX 01	

Project	Alfred Pinkus and Jonny Roberts	Date Prepared:	28-Apr-73
Project Manager:	Mary Johnson	Project Customer:	Professor Zakari

Purpose

The plan defines how risks associated with TMX 01 project will be identified, analyzed and mitigated. It will establish a platform on how risk management activities will be performed, recorded as well as monitored. Risk register will be established with this plan for new risk identification, risk prioritization and risks response.

Risk Management Procedure and Approaches

Mary Johnson together with the project team member and Alfred Pinkus & Jonny Roberts will ensure that risks are identified, analyzed, and managed throughout the life cycle of the TMX 01 project. They will ensure risks are identified as early as possible to mitigate their impact.

Risk Identification

All the stakeholders will be involved to identify new risk. When ever any risk will be identified, it will be documented in risk register and will be notified in status meeting to all stakeholders. Attention should be given to the deliverables, assumptions, constraints, WBS, estimates, resources to identify new risk.

Risk Prioritization and Analysis

Mary Johnson will assess the range of possible project outcomes. Qualification will be used to identify top rated risks to track, respond and ignore. The probability and impact of occurrence for each identified risk will be assessed by Mary Johnson with support of all the team members.
Probability and impact matrix criteria:

Probability
High – Probability of occurrence is greater than 80%
Medium – Probability of occurrence is between 20% and 80%
Low – Probability of occurrence is below 20%

Impact
High – Greatly impact project cost, project schedule or performance
Medium – Slight or medium impact project cost, project schedule or performance
Low – Little impact on cost, schedule or performance

After qualitative risk analysis Mary Johnson will do quantitative risk analysis for high priority risk to analyze the impact on time, cost and performance and will present in status meeting.

Risk Management plan

Each major risk will be assigned to a project team member for monitoring purposes and they will be responsible to present status of the risk to Mary Johnson every week. For positive or negative risks Mary Johnson will decide the final response approach after discussion of team members. For positive risk approaches should be exploit, enhance, share or accept whereas for negative risks approaches should be avoid, mitigate, transfer or accept.

Risk Monitor and Control

All the risks involved in Wedding Bell of James & Mary project will be regularly monitored and controlled throughout the project lifecycle according to their priority. Any change requests will be analyzed for their possible impact to the project risks. Program manager will be notified of important changes to risk status.

Tools and Techniques

Risk Register will be maintained by the Mary Johnson and will be reviewed and updated on every project team meetings.

Risk Name	Qualitative Rating				Risk Response	
	Probability	Impact	Risk Score	Risk Ranking	Risk Response	Risk Owner
Project cancelled	Medium	High	24.6	1	Not	Not finalized
Scope creep	High	Low	18	2	Not	Not finalized
Scope change	High	Low	13.86	3	Not	Not finalized
Project date change	High	Low	12.58	3	Not	Not finalized
Project duration changed	High	Low	13.3	3	Not	Not finalized
Budget limit exceed	High	Medium	24.2	1	Not	Not finalized
Obtaining discount	Medium	Low	9.3	4	Watch list	Not finalized
Low quality work like design, programming etc.	Medium	Medium	17.49	2	Not	Not finalized
Previous phase low quality impact on current phase	Medium	Low	5.44	5	Watch list	Not finalized
Quality standard changed	Medium	Medium	10	3	Not	Not finalized

Approvals

Project Manager Signature		Sponsor or Originator Signature	
Project Manager Name		Sponsor or Originator Name	
Date		Date	

Form 26: Risk Management Plan

21   Identify Risks

The Identify Risks process determines which risks may affect the project and their characteristics. Participants in this process should include all project personnel: Project Manager, team members, risk management team assigned, customers, subject matter experts (SMEs), end users, stakeholders and risk management experts. This is an iterative process which may have to be done as the project moves through its life-cycle and as new risks emerge.

Inputs	Tools and Techniques	Outputs
◦ Risk management plan ◦ Cost management plan ◦ Schedule management plan ◦ Quality management plan ◦ Human resource management plan ◦ Scope baseline ◦ Activity cost estimates ◦ Activity duration estimates ◦ Stakeholder register ◦ Project documents ◦ Procurement documents ◦ Enterprise environmental factors ◦ Organizational process assets	◦ Documentation reviews ◦ Information gathering techniques ◦ Checklist analysis ◦ Assumptions analysis ◦ Diagramming techniques ◦ SWOT analysis ◦ Expert judgment	◦ Risk register

Figure 26: Identify Risks: Inputs, Tools & Techniques and Outputs

Risk Register

The Risk Register is a detailed document with all the identified project risks and potential risk responses. The Risk Register is a living document which is updated throughout the project with current risk-related information once it is created. In the initial stages it could contain:

• List of identified risks: describing risks in detail. If event A occurs, it will cause Event B leading to Effect C.

- *Root causes of risks which should be documented and used to support subsequent risk identification in current and future projects.*
- *Risk owners who will be responsible for managing each identified risk and deducing a relevant response in the Plan Risk Responses process. The risk owner is different from the risk response owner who carries out the risk response later in the project.*
- *List of potential responses: potential responses to risks could be identified in the identify risks process and used as an input during the Plan Risk Responses process.*

22 Perform Qualitative Risk Analysis

The Perform Qualitative Risk Analysis process is typically a rapid means of prioritizing risks. This prioritization should be revisited through the project's life-cycle to be updated with changes in project risks or new risks. The Perform Qualitative Risk Analysis process involves prioritizing identified risks in order for further actions. This "further action" occurs within the Perform Quantitative Risk Analysis and the Plan Risk Responses processes. Factors considered in Qualitative Risk Analysis include:

- Time frame for the risk and risk tolerance.
- Constraints of cost, schedule and quality.
- Relative probability of occurrences.
- Organization's risk tolerance.
- Managing risk attitudes of key participants.

Establishing definitions for the levels of probability and impact to reduce bias: what determines a risk being categorized as low, medium or high rather than just throwing out a number.

Inputs	Tools and Techniques	Outputs
• Risk management plan • Scope baseline • Risk register • Enterprise environmental factors • Organizational process assets	• Risk probability and impact assessment • Probability and impact matrix • Risk data quality assessment • Risk categorization • Risk urgency assessment • Expert judgment	• Project documents updates

Figure 27: Perform Qualitative Risk Analysis: Inputs, Tools & Techniques and Outputs

23 Perform Quantitative Risk Analysis

The Perform Quantitative Risk Analysis process is performed on prioritized risks (from the Perform Qualitative Risk Analysis process) which are viewed as being able to substantially impact the project's competing demands. This process analyzes the effect of such risk events on the project by assigning a monetary value to the impact of those risks and thereby presenting a quantitative approach to decision making risk management. The Project Manager and team evaluate and consider the aggregate effect of all risks affecting the project thereby providing a quantitative approach to making project decisions where there is uncertainty.

Inputs	Tools and Techniques	Outputs
<ul><li>Risk Management Plan</li><li>Cost management plan</li><li>Schedule management plan</li><li>Risk register</li><li>Enterprise environmental factors</li><li>Organizational Process Assets</li></ul>	<ul><li>Data Gathering and representation techniques</li><li>Quantitative risk analysis and modeling techniques</li><li>Expert judgment</li></ul>	<ul><li>Project documents updates</li></ul>

Figure 28: Perform Quantitative Risk Analysis: Inputs, Tools & Techniques and Outputs

24 Plan Risk Responses

The Plan Risk Responses process involves developing a plan of action and options to enhance opportunities and reduce threats to project objectives. The risk owners play a prominent role in this process by proposing responses on how to manage identified risks.

In this process, risks are addressed by their priority. Resources and activities are planned into the schedule, budget and Project Management Plan as necessary. This process also involves the identification and assignment of risk response owners (also known as risk action owners) to implement each agreed to and funded risk response. Planned risk responses should be appropriate to the magnitude of the risk.

Inputs	Tools and Techniques	Outputs
• Risk Management Plan • Risk Register	• Strategies for negative risks or threats • Strategies for positive risks or opportunities • Contingent response strategies • Expert judgment	• Project management plan updates • Project documents updates

Figure 29: Plan Risk Responses: Inputs, Tools & Techniques and Outputs

Risk Register

Project Title: TMX 01

Project Sponsor:	Alfred Pinkus and Jonny Roberts
Project Manager:	Mary Johnson
Date Prepared:	28-Apr-73
Project Customer:	Professor Zakari

	Identify risks			Perform Qualitative Risk Analysis			Perform Quantitative Risk Analysis			Plan Risk Responses			Control Risks
ID	CAUSE	RISK	EFFECT	PROBABILITY RATING (1 - 5)	IMPACT RATING (1 - 5)	RISK SCORE	PROBABILITY	IMPACT($)	EMV ($)	STRATEGY	RISK OWNER	RISK ACTION ITEM OWNERS	STATUS
1	Speed of schedule and budget	Lack of Defense Permits	Potential fines, discontinuation	5	3	15	2	$ 5,000,000.00	$ 10,000,000.00	AVOID	Mary	Andrew	CLOSED
2	No formal plan or detail drawings for intricate deliverables	Inadequate mechanical, science, bio-tech and power requirements	Additional unknown cost and/or delay	3	4	12	0.5	$ 4,000,000.00	$ 2,000,000.00	AVOID	Bill	Max	OPEN
3	Improper research, and planning	Inadequate Weaponry on Arrival (Future)	Bodily harm, injury or death. Loss of TMX to hostile future earthlings	4	4	16	0.6	$ 150,000,000,000.00	$ 90,000,000,000.00	AVOID	Pinkus	Alan	CLOSED
4	Lack of stakeholder engagement	Understanding the effect of project on other stakeholders	Rework, redesign &/or disgruntled employees	4	2	8	0.8	$ 3,000,000.00	$ 2,400,000.00	MITIGATE	Zakari	Maria	OPEN
5	Proper planning and inspections	Humgus 2 virus may afflict time travellers	Illness, disease, time, cost etc	1	4	4	0.02	$ 140,000,000.00	$ 2,800,000.00	ACCEPT	Jimmy	Ney	CLOSED
6	Improper programming	Harm to testing specimen (Chimp or other)	Death, PETA fines, bad publicity, project abandonment	4	1	4	0.8	$ 200.00	160.00	MITIGATE	Lynn	Thyro	OPEN
7	No advance planning	Computer & IT services under capacity.	Additional unknown cost and/or delay	3	1	3	0.6	$ 5,000.00	$ 3,000.00	AVOID	Johnny	Oh-Jin	CLOSED
									$ 90,017,203,160.00				

Form 27: Risk Register

25 Plan Procurement Management

The Plan Procurement Management process involves documenting project purchasing decisions and specifying the process for procuring deliverables (products, services or results) outside the performing organization. In this process the team identifies deliverables which can best be or must be met by an external party and those that can be met internally.

The team decides what to purchase, why to purchase it and how much is needed (for example how many additional resources). The team also makes "make or buy" decisions and considers potential sellers. The team should also consider the responsibility for holding professional licenses and permits required for the project. The project schedule is a major input when planning procurements because the timing of procurements should align with the planned work periods and deliverable completion dates.

Inputs	Tools and Techniques	Outputs
Project management plan		Procurement management plan
Requirements documentation		Procurement statement of work
Risk register	Make-or-buy analysis	Procurement documents
Activity resource requirements	Expert judgment	Source selection criteria
Project schedule	Market research	Make-or-buy decisions
Activity cost estimates	Meetings	Change requests
Stakeholder register		Project documents updates
Enterprise environmental factors		
Organizational process assets		

Figure 30: Plan Procurement Management: Inputs, Tools & Techniques and Outputs

Procurement Management Plan

Project Title:		TMX 01		

Project Sponsor:	Alfred	Date Prepared:	23-Jun-33
Project Manager:	Mary	Project Customer:	Professor Zakari

What needs to be purchased (People, Services, Product, Results, etc.)	Contract Type						Lead Time Required	Constraints and/or Assumptions	Prequalified Sellers
	FFP	FPIF	CPIF	CPFF	CPPC	T&M			
Time Travel adaptation training	X						28 weeks	Unknowns	Zenickthe Consulting Inc.
Carbon ZX1 Polymer		X					20 weeks	Government restrictions of new compound	JLD Ltd
Bar-34H36 X Contact			X				17 weeks	Government restrictions of new compound	Aero Naunt Partners
Work on remote station		X					20 weeks	None	Zarago Brothers
Venus Staff augmentation Team				X			20 weeks	Skill levels do not currently exist. Training included.	Pentious Nandous
Polycarbonate Giga Fiber						X	64 weeks	Schedule delays 20% expected based on FW reputation.	Flight-Wing
Steel Weld Dev. Sub-Project						X	90 weeks	Permit for STGD651080-Z	London Steel Inc.
D&B Lab Annex					X		52 weeks	Weather delays expected to offset schedule by 5%	USN- Construction Inc.
Agency Lobby & Cultural Initiative		X					16 weeks	None	Commco Inc.
SW024 Tanganium-Oxide Material						X	20 weeks	New material - Govt regulation issue.	Flight-Wing

Form 28: Procurement Management Plan

26 Plan Stakeholder Management

In Plan Stakeholder Management, the key goal is to develop a strategy for keeping stakeholders engaged while meeting their needs. The Project Manager should intentionally strategize how to keep stakeholders engaged on the project. The real benefit of going through this in a deliberate way is to develop a clear plan on how to get the stakeholders on the project engaged and focused, pulling them in at the right time. The key output from this process is the Stakeholder Management Plan.

Inputs	Tools and Techniques	Outputs
Project management plan Requirements documentation Risk register Activity resource requirements Project schedule Activity cost estimates Stakeholder register Enterprise environmental factors Organizational process assets	Make-or-buy analysis Expert judgment Market research Meetings	Procurement management plan Procurement statement of work Procurement documents Source selection criteria Make-or-buy decisions Change requests Project documents updates

Figure 31: Plan Procurement Management: Inputs, Tools & Techniques and Outputs

Stakeholder Management Plan

The Stakeholder Management Plan defines how stakeholder engagement and expectations will be managed on the project. It could be summarized or broad. It identifies the management strategies required to effectively engage stakeholders. Additional details contained in this plan could include:

- Desired and current engagement levels of key stakeholders (as seen in a Stakeholder Engagement Assessment Matrix)
- Scope and impact of change to stakeholders
- Identified interrelationships and potential overlap between stakeholders
- Stakeholder communication requirements for the current project phase
- Method for updating and refining the Stakeholder Management Plan

Planning Conclusion

The planning process group consists of several different processes to develop the final project management plan. This is a collection of several of the baselines and subsidiary plans talked about in this section.

Though covered in under 7 minutes in the corresponding DVD, this could be a rather arduous endeavor taking months and in some cases years for the team to put together.

After developing the Project Management Plan, and you have direction for the planning processing group, you move into the next Process Group which is executing.

Bear in mind; while you are developing the Project Management Plan, there are actually several things that happen. It's not quite as clear cut and as easy as performing several processes in sequence. In reality there is lots of overlap between all the planning processes of project management throughout the project and for the life of the project. The same applies to all other Process Groups.

Group Discussion
Briefly discuss the processes of project management pertaining to the following:
1. Collecting requirements
2. In which document is the project scope described in easily understood terms.
3. How to create a WBS.
4. How to develop a schedule.
5. How to determine the project budget.
6. What to consider when planning for quality.
7. Components of the Human Resource Plan that impact the budget.
8. Why the Project Manager should plan for communications.
9. What the team should be aware of when planning for risks.
10. Activities you would expect to occur in procurement management.
11. What is a Stakeholder Management Plan?

Planning Process Group Real-World Project Work

a) Describe how you would manage requirements gathering on your project from start to finish. Which tools or templates would you use?

b) Using your requirements traceability matrix, map out 3 requirements to their origin indicating validation terms and responsibilities.

c) Create a Level 2 WBS of your current project assigning a code of accounts to each level.

d) Decompose one arm of your WBS down to a 40 hour Work package level.

e) On a blank sheet, decompose a work-package down to the activity level. Each activity could be 8 hours or less. At the end of this exercise you should have an activity list of 5 - 10 activities. Give each activity a special identifier. This could be a code such as A1, A2 or anything else you feel is relevant to your specific project.

f) Arrange the activities from your activity list in order of occurrence. Indicate the duration for each activity in workdays or hours.

g) Estimate the type and quantity of resources available and needed to complete your list of activities.

h) Decide on a start date for the first activity and create a rough schedule for your listed activities.

i) Make a high-level estimate for all your activities.

j) Add up your individual estimates to a final total.

k) Complete your Quality Management Plan at a high-level. Briefly describe your quality assurance, quality control and process improvement approach.

l) Complete the following sections in your Human Resource plan template:
- Roles, Responsibilities, and Authority
- Staff Acquisition and Staff release
- Training needs
- Rewards and recognition & Safety

m) Complete your Communications Management Plan at a high-level. Briefly describe 3 messages that will be conveyed on the project indicating: Audience, Method, Frequency and Sender.

n) Complete your risk management plan describing: Methods and Approaches, Roles and Responsibilities and Risk Categories.

o) Identify 3 negative risks and 2 positive risks on your project.

p) Qualitatively analyze the negative risks using your Probability and Impact Matrix. Assign a risk score to each negative risk and further categorize the risks as high-medium or low.

q) Attempt to quantitatively analyze the negative risks.

r) Plan how you will respond to each risk. Which strategy will you employ to deal with each risk?

s) Decide with your team members what to make and what to buy on your project. Give reasons for needing to buy anything.

SECTION 6

EXECUTING THE
PROJECT MANAGEMENT PLAN

Now the plan has been developed, in order to execute the planned project work the team needs the project management plan. It is the role of the project manager to ensure that the work is executed according to the plan. The project manager may work with functional managers on the project team to ensure that work being carried out is performed according to the plan and the right quality standards.

In the Executing process group, the project manager executes the project management plan, putting it into action. In executing, this is where the work is carried out, and the project manager ensures any approved changes are implemented as requested. This is where the project team checks the work processes for correctness. This is known as quality assurance.

Other tasks that happen in this process group include:

- Managing the project work by integrating all moving parts being executed
- Acquiring the project team.
- Developing the project team.
- Managing the project team.
- Managing stakeholder expectations.
- Awarding a contract to vendors working on the project.
- Coordinating all efforts aimed at directing and managing the ongoing project work.

There is a lot of work to be done in this process group even though in the Executing process group, there are fewer than half of the processes in the planning process group!

Very little or no documentation is created here. Rather information for the documents created in planning is updated. These are referred to as project management plan updates and project documents updates.

Let's review some of the process carried out during this process.

27   Direct and Manage Project Work

The Direct and Manage Project Work process involves directing and managing the execution of project work defined in the Project Management Plan to meet requirements defined in the Project Scope Statement. Other activities *coordinated* in this process include:

- Performing the work documented in the Project Management Plan to achieve project objectives and produce deliverables.

- Acquiring human and equipment resources.

- Training the Project Team.

- Implementing methods and standards.

- Generating project data, project reports, status and progress information used for forecasting.

- Managing risks and implementing risk response activities.

- Managing seller and supplier contractual relationships.

Collecting work performance information which is fed into several Monitoring and Controlling Process Group processes.

Inputs	Tools and Techniques	Outputs
Project management plan Approved change requests Enterprise environmental factors Organization process assets	Expert judgment Project management information system Meetings	Deliverables Work performance data Change requests Project management plan updates Project documents updates

Figure 32: Direct and Manage Project Work: Inputs, Tools & Techniques and Outputs

Change Request

Project Title:	TMX 01
Requester:	Max Planck
Requested date:	15-Mar-79

Description

Combat prototype is a new invention at Dec-78 which can serve better than Rapid prototype because it provides option to reduce time by 6 months with only USD 100,000 incremental costs.

Reason

Time savings in acquiring necessary techniques that is not present in the Rapid prototype.

Change Category

Scope	▓	Yes		No
Schedule	▓	Yes		No
Cost	▓	Yes		No
Quality		Yes	▓	No
Deliverables	▓	Yes		No
Resources	▓	Yes		No

Change Affect

Corrective Action		Yes	▓	No
Preventive Action	▓	Yes		No
Defect Repair		Yes	▓	No

Alternative Consideration

Noveau Inconnu can purchase the idea used last year at Combat prototype or purchase a service from Fruence Indico in 3 weeks notice.

Other Change requirements

N/A

Risk

Risk of Combat prototype not working backwards time travel feature which can lead to waste of time and money.

Estimation

Cost	USD 100,000
Resources	2

Approval

▓		Approved
		Rejected

Justification	It provides opportunity to have good impact in the project with minimal

Form 29: Change Request

28 Perform Quality Assurance

The Perform Quality Assurance process involves the application of planned and systematic activities to provide confidence to customers and stakeholders that quality standards are being met. It involves auditing the quality requirements, results and measurements from the Control Quality process to ensure application of appropriate quality standards and operational definitions.

The Perform Quality Assurance process is a way of achieving continuous process improvement which involves iterative improvements of quality to eliminate redundant, non value-added activities. It is also aimed at eliminating waste thereby increasing work efficiency and process effectiveness.

The Perform Quality Assurance process involves monitoring and documenting specific project results to verify if they comply with the relevant quality standards and identifying ways to eliminate causes of unsatisfactory performance by identifying and controlling deviation from quality.

Inputs	Tools and Techniques	Outputs
<ul><li>Quality management plan</li><li>Process improvement plan</li><li>Quality metrics</li><li>Quality control measurements</li><li>Project documents</li></ul>	<ul><li>Quality management and control tools</li><li>Quality audits</li><li>Process analysis</li></ul>	<ul><li>Change requests</li><li>Project management plan updates</li><li>Project documents updates</li><li>Organizational process assets updates</li></ul>

Figure 33: Perform Quality Assurance: Inputs, Tools & Techniques and Outputs

29   Acquire Project Team

The Acquire Project Team process involves acquiring the Project Team that is responsible for completing project deliverables. This occurs during the Executing Process Group and is based on project requirements determined during planning. On large projects all the Project Team may not have been acquired during planning although majority of the project management team responsible for planning may have. It is not uncommon to have to plan a project without the whole Project Team. In some projects during the course of executing, resources may be pulled into other projects or resources that the project hinged on may have moved on. Acquiring additional resources is not uncommon.

The Project Manager and project management team should influence others in a position to release resources for the project (e.g. functional managers). Highlighting benefits to the organization and the experience that resources could gain is a good way of gaining buy-in from functional heads when seeking participation of their team members on projects.

Inability to acquire the required human resources could impact the project schedule, budget, scope and quality of the project and its deliverables. If assumptions are made around certain very skilled or senior team members being available, then it is essential that personnel of that staff level are available to fulfill project roles and responsibilities. Potential unavailability of planned resources should be flagged as a project risk.

Inputs	Tools and Techniques	Outputs
• Human resource management plan • Enterprise environmental factors • Organizational process assets	• Pre-assignment • Negotiation • Acquisition • Virtual teams • Multi-criteria decision analysis	• Project staff assignments • Resource calendars • Project Management plan updates

Figure 34: Acquire Project Team: Inputs, Tools & Techniques and Outputs

30 Develop Project Team

Developing the Project Team involves activities which enhance the Project Team's performance and interaction such as team building and training to equip them with skills necessary to complete project activities. Examples of effective team work are: sharing unbalanced workloads, communicating and sharing information.

It is the responsibility of the Project Manager to identify, build, motivate, lead and inspire the team through skill assessment, training, team building, presenting opportunities and challenges while boosting the team's morale in situations that demand it.

The Project Manager is also responsible to:

- Acquire resources needed to develop an effective project management team.

- Improve knowledge and skills of the team to enable them better complete deliverables, fulfill their obligations and meet required project objectives.

- Improve trust and agreement levels among the team in order to boost morale and increase productivity.

- Create a cohesive team culture to improve team spirit cooperation and productivity.

- Promote cross-training and mentoring between team
  members to enable expertise and knowledge share.

Inputs	Tools and Techniques	Outputs
◦ Human resource management plan ◦ Project staff assignments ◦ Resource calendars	◦ Interpersonal skills ◦ Training ◦ Team-building activities ◦ Ground rules ◦ Colocation ◦ Recognition and rewards ◦ Personnel assessment tools	◦ Team performance assessments ◦ Enterprise environmental factors updates

Figure 35: Develop Project Team: Inputs, Tools & Techniques and Outputs

Team Member Performance Assessment

Project Title:	TMX 01		
Project Sponsor:	Alfred Pinkus and Jonny Roberts	Date Prepared:	25-Jul-73
Project Manager:	Mary Johnson	Project Customer:	Professor Zakari

Introduction

This assessment is developed to manage performance assessment system for project team members to provide fair and objective assessment within TMX01 project that promotes objectivity and measurability of performance expectations.

Performance Assessment

Team Member Name	Andrew				

Technical Performance Review

Criteria	Weight				
	5	4	3	2	1
Scope	Outstanding	Exceed Expectation	Meet Expectation	Need improvement	Did not meet Expectation
Comments (For Weight 5 & 1 only):					
Schedule	Outstanding	Exceed Expectation	Meet Expectation	Need improvement	Did not meet Expectation
Comments (For Weight 5 & 1 only):					
Cost	Outstanding	Exceed Expectation	Meet Expectation	Need improvement	Did not meet Expectation
Comments (For Weight 5 & 1 only):					
Quality	Outstanding	Exceed Expectation	Meet Expectation	Need improvement	Did not meet Expectation
Comments (For Weight 5 & 1 only):					

Interpersonal Competency Review

Criteria	Weight				
	5	4	3	2	1
Leadership	Outstanding	Exceed Expectation	Meet Expectation	Need improvement	Did not meet Expectation
Comments (For Weight 5 & 1 only):					
Communication	Outstanding	Exceed Expectation	Meet Expectation	Need improvement	Did not meet Expectation
Comments (For Weight 5 & 1 only):					
Decision Making	Outstanding	Exceed Expectation	Meet Expectation	Need improvement	Did not meet Expectation
Comments (For Weight 5 & 1 only):					
Problem Solving	Outstanding	Exceed Expectation	Meet Expectation	Need improvement	Did not meet Expectation
Comments (For Weight 5 & 1 only):					
Conflict Management	Outstanding	Exceed Expectation	Meet Expectation	Need improvement	Did not meet Expectation
Comments (For Weight 5 & 1 only):					

Team Member Performance Assessment

Development program

Area	Action Plan
Decision Making	Training
Problem Solving	Training

Team Member Name	Henry				

Technical Performance Review

Criteria	Weight				
	5	4	3	2	1
Scope	Outstanding	Exceed Expectation	Meet Expectation	Need improvement	Did not meet Expectation
Comments (For Weight 5 & 1 only):					
Schedule	Outstanding	Exceed Expectation	Meet Expectation	Need improvement	Did not meet Expectation
Comments (For Weight 5 & 1 only):					
Cost	Outstanding	Exceed Expectation	Meet Expectation	Need improvement	Did not meet Expectation
Comments (For Weight 5 & 1 only):					
Quality	Outstanding	Exceed Expectation	Meet Expectation	Need improvement	Did not meet Expectation
Comments (For Weight 5 & 1 only): Provided outstanding quality assurance support to detect process failure and provided recommendation that was a					

Interpersonal Competency Review

Criteria	Weight				
	5	4	3	2	1
Leadership	Outstanding	Exceed Expectation	Meet Expectation	Need improvement	Did not meet Expectation
Comments (For Weight 5 & 1 only):					
Communication	Outstanding	Exceed Expectation	Meet Expectation	Need improvement	Did not meet Expectation
Comments (For Weight 5 & 1 only):					
Decision Making	Outstanding	Exceed Expectation	Meet Expectation	Need improvement	Did not meet Expectation
Comments (For Weight 5 & 1 only):					
Problem Solving	Outstanding	Exceed Expectation	Meet Expectation	Need improvement	Did not meet Expectation
Comments (For Weight 5 & 1 only):					
Conflict Management	Outstanding	Exceed Expectation	Meet Expectation	Need improvement	Did not meet Expectation
Comments (For Weight 5 & 1 only):					

Team Member Performance Assessment

Development program

Area	Action Plan
Conflict Management	Training

Team Member Name	Ney Dimaculangan

Technical Performance Review

Criteria	Weight				
	5	4	3	2	1
Scope	Outstanding	[x] Exceed Expectation	Meet Expectation	Need improvement	Did not meet Expectation
Comments (For Weight 5 & 1 only):					
Schedule	Outstanding	Exceed Expectation	[x] Meet Expectation	Need improvement	Did not meet Expectation
Comments (For Weight 5 & 1 only):					
Cost	Outstanding	Exceed Expectation	[x] Meet Expectation	Need improvement	Did not meet Expectation
Comments (For Weight 5 & 1 only):					
Quality	Outstanding	Exceed Expectation	Meet Expectation	[x] Need improvement	Did not meet Expectation
Comments (For Weight 5 & 1 only):					

Interpersonal Competency Review

Criteria	Weight				
	5	4	3	2	1
Leadership	Outstanding	Exceed Expectation	Meet Expectation	[x] Need improvement	Did not meet Expectation
Comments (For Weight 5 & 1 only):					
Communication	Outstanding	Exceed Expectation	[x] Meet Expectation	Need improvement	Did not meet Expectation
Comments (For Weight 5 & 1 only):					
Decision Making	Outstanding	Exceed Expectation	[x] Meet Expectation	Need improvement	Did not meet Expectation
Comments (For Weight 5 & 1 only):					
Problem Solving	Outstanding	Exceed Expectation	[x] Meet Expectation	Need improvement	Did not meet Expectation
Comments (For Weight 5 & 1 only):					
Conflict Management	Outstanding	[x] Exceed Expectation	Meet Expectation	Need improvement	Did not meet Expectation
Comments (For Weight 5 & 1 only):					

Team Member Performance Assessment

Development program

Area	Action Plan
Quality	Attain seminar of QoS team
Leadership	Training

Team Member Name	Natalya Antyukh

Technical Performance Review

Criteria	Weight				
	5	4	3	2	1
Scope	Outstanding	[x] Exceed Expectation	Meet Expectation	Need improvement	Did not meet Expectation
Comments (For Weight 5 & 1 only):					
Schedule	Outstanding	Exceed Expectation	[x] Meet Expectation	Need improvement	Did not meet Expectation
Comments (For Weight 5 & 1 only):					
Cost	Outstanding	[x] Exceed Expectation	Meet Expectation	Need improvement	Did not meet Expectation
Comments (For Weight 5 & 1 only):					
Quality	Outstanding	[x] Exceed Expectation	Meet Expectation	Need improvement	Did not meet Expectation
Comments (For Weight 5 & 1 only):					

Interpersonal Competency Review

Team Member Performance Assessment

Development program

Area	Action Plan	
Decision Making	Training	
Problem Solving	Training	

Team Member Name	Alan Turing

Technical Performance Review

Criteria	Weight				
	5	4	3	2	1
Scope	Outstanding	Exceed Expectation	Meet Expectation	Need improvement	Did not meet Expectation
Comments (For Weight 5 & 1 only):					
Schedule	Outstanding	Exceed Expectation	Meet Expectation	Need improvement	Did not meet Expectation
Comments (For Weight 5 & 1 only):					
Cost	Outstanding	Exceed Expectation	Meet Expectation	Need improvement	Did not meet Expectation
Comments (For Weight 5 & 1 only):					
Quality	Outstanding	Exceed Expectation	Meet Expectation	Need improvement	Did not meet Expectation
Comments (For Weight 5 & 1 only): Provided outstanding quality assurance support to detect process failure and provided recommendation that was a					

Interpersonal Competency Review

Criteria	Weight				
	5	4	3	2	1
Leadership	Outstanding	Exceed Expectation	Meet Expectation	Need improvement	Did not meet Expectation
Comments (For Weight 5 & 1 only):					
Communication	Outstanding	Exceed Expectation	Meet Expectation	Need improvement	Did not meet Expectation
Comments (For Weight 5 & 1 only):					
Decision Making	Outstanding	Exceed Expectation	Meet Expectation	Need improvement	Did not meet Expectation
Comments (For Weight 5 & 1 only):					
Problem Solving	Outstanding	Exceed Expectation	Meet Expectation	Need improvement	Did not meet Expectation
Comments (For Weight 5 & 1 only):					
Conflict Management	Outstanding	Exceed Expectation	Meet Expectation	Need improvement	Did not meet Expectation
Comments (For Weight 5 & 1 only):					

Team Member Performance Assessment

Development program

Area	Action Plan	
Conflict Management	Training	

Team Member Name	Sally Pearson

Technical Performance Review

Criteria	Weight				
	5	4	3	2	1
Scope	Outstanding	Exceed Expectation	Meet Expectation	Need improvement	Did not meet Expectation
Comments (For Weight 5 & 1 only):					
Schedule	Outstanding	Exceed Expectation	Meet Expectation	Need improvement	Did not meet Expectation
Comments (For Weight 5 & 1 only):					
Cost	Outstanding	Exceed Expectation	Meet Expectation	Need improvement	Did not meet Expectation
Comments (For Weight 5 & 1 only):					
Quality	Outstanding	Exceed Expectation	Meet Expectation	Need improvement	Did not meet Expectation
Comments (For Weight 5 & 1 only):					

Interpersonal Competency Review

Criteria	Weight				
	5	4	3	2	1
Leadership	Outstanding	Exceed Expectation	Meet Expectation	Need improvement	Did not meet Expectation
Comments (For Weight 5 & 1 only):					
Communication	Outstanding	Exceed Expectation	Meet Expectation	Need improvement	Did not meet Expectation

Form 30: Team Performance Assessment

31 Manage Project Team

This involves tracking team member performance by observing the team, conducting project performance appraisals and managing issue logs to track and resolve issues as well as manage conflict. It also involves providing feedback and managing changes to optimize project performance. As a result of managing the Project Team, change requests may be submitted and the Human Resource Plan updated.

Information is provided from performance appraisals and lessons learned are added to the organization's databases.

Inputs	Tools and Techniques	Outputs
• Human resource management plan • Project staff assignments • Team performance assessments • Issue log • Work performance reports • Organizational process assets	• Observation and conversation • Project performance appraisals • Conflict management • Interpersonal skills	• Change requests • Project management plan updates • Project documents updates • Enterprise environmental factors updates • Organizational process assets updates

Figure 36: Manage Project Team: Inputs, Tools & Techniques and Outputs

32 Manage Communications

This involves making project information available to project stakeholders in a timely manner. It entails implementing the Communications Management Plan and responding to unexpected requests for information. To effectively Manage Communications, the Project Manager should consider:

- Sender-receiver models.
- Choice of media – verbal vs. email or report.
- Writing style – word choice and structure.
- Meeting management techniques – agendas and conflicts.
- Presentation techniques – body language and visual aids.

Facilitation techniques – building consensus and overcoming challenges.

Inputs	Tools and Techniques	Outputs
Communications management plan Work performance reports Enterprise environmental factors Organizational process assets	Communication technology Communication models Communication methods Information management systems Performance reporting	Project communications Project management plan updates Project document updates Organizational process assets updates

Figure 37: Manage Communications: Inputs, Tools & Techniques and Outputs

33 Conduct Procurements

The Conduct Procurements process involves sending out procurement documents and obtaining responses from sellers (quotations, bids, offers or proposals) and details on how project requirements can be met. Procurement requests are issued based on company policies which may include publicizing the request via newspaper, trade journals, and public registries or via the internet.

In this process, the team decides who the project will be awarded to by reviewing offers and making a selection among potential sellers. The team is also involved in the following activities:

- Obtaining seller information.
- Establishing a negotiating sequence by ranking proposals by weighted evaluation scores assigned to each proposal.
- Screening the initial list to obtain a shortlist and more details from sellers after which a weighting system can be applied.
- Applying previously defined selection criteria to select
  sellers who are qualified and suitable to perform the project work.
- Negotiating written contracts with the selected sellers.
- Selecting a seller.
- Awarding a contract.

Inputs	Tools and Techniques	Outputs
Procurement management plan Procurement documents Source selection criteria Seller proposals Project documents Make-or-buy decisions Procurement statement of work Organizational process assets	Bidder conferences Proposal evaluation techniques Independent estimates Expert judgment Advertising Analytical techniques Procurement negotiations	Selected sellers Agreements Resource calendars Change requests Project management plan updates Project documents updates

Figure 38: Conduct Procurements: Inputs, Tools & Techniques and Outputs

34 Manage Stakeholder Engagement

Manage Stakeholder Engagement involves collaborating with stakeholders to meet their needs and address any issues as they arise. It involves increasing stakeholder support and minimizing resistance.

In order to Manage Stakeholder Engagement on a project, the Project Manager should be proactive by pulling in stakeholders at the right time, ensuring that they receive necessary project information to make key decisions and be as engaged as possible.

Inputs	Tools and Techniques	Outputs
Stakeholder Management Plan Communications Management Plan Change Log Organizational process assets	Communication Methods Interpersonal Skills Management Skills	Issue Log Change Requests Project management Plan Updates Project Documents Updates Organizational Process Assets Updates

Figure 39: Manage Stakeholder Engagement: Inputs, Tools & Techniques and Outputs

Executing Process Group Summary

In summary, executing a project involves several feedback loops with other processes especially those in the Monitoring and Controlling area. This is where work processes are undertaken to produce the deliverable. In the next chapter, we will be discussing what happens next after the deliverable is sent for an inspection by the performing organization (this is called quality control). The project deliverable is also sent to the customer for inspection and approval in a process known as "Verify Scope". A characteristic of the Executing Process Group worth noting is this is where majority of the project resources are spent.

Group Discussion
Briefly discuss what it means to execute the Project Management Plan and activities you would expect to occur in this Process Group.

Executing Process Group Real-World Project Work

a. **Change Request**

Your client has just informed you of some critical changes to the project requirements. These changes will involve some customizations for this client. Complete a Change Request to submit to the Change Control Board within your organization for review and approval.

b. **Change Log**

You have been tracking all changes to the project from client requests as well as changes from other internal organizational departments. Complete a Change Log for the change request you submitted (in the previous exercise), tracking it through final disposition.

c. **Decision Log**

You have been tracking all the major decisions that were made on the project, who made them, and when they were made. Complete a Decision Log showing 3 important decisions made as well as the alternatives considered in managing your project.

d. **Quality Audit**

The QA task owner had just completed audits on the project when your client's recent change requests were approved. This caused some rework for your QA contact and he/she finally completed the audit yesterday. QA found some discrepancy between what was already in the system and the new changes you made. For instance, the fee per report, the frequency of the report as well as the type of report all need to be changed due to new customizations for the client. Based on these findings, complete a Quality Audit form, showing information you would expect to receive from QA following this audit.

e. **Team Operating Agreement**

Your new project is comprised of virtual team members from your organization as well as members from different organizations. Complete a Team Operating Agreement to establish ground rules and guidelines for the team.

f. **Issue Log**

You have been keeping track of all open issues that are in question or that are not settled on the project. Complete an Issue Log showing 2 major issues under discussion.

Chapter 8: Down to Business

Several months later after the team had completed all up-front planning, front end engineering and risk analysis, Billy and Mary walked hurriedly down the vast corridor deep within the "skunk works" of Noveau Inconnu toward the next project management meeting.

"I don't know, Bill, did we make the right choice? I mean, a Time Machine? Yes, the potential return on investment is huge, but a Time Machine? Is such a thing even possible?"

"That's why Pinkus called this meeting here in R&D," Billy replied, "so we can hear what the engineers and science geeks have to say. From the buzz I've heard so far, most of them agree that Zakari is a weird old bird, but he's definitely a genius."

They arrived at the door to the main conference room in R&D. Mary gazed into the biometric scanner. The light on the lock cycled green. Just before entering the room, Mary turned to Bill and said, "You know what I can't wrap my head around, Bill? If we are successful and build the darn thing, wouldn't that mean that people from the future would already be visiting us back here?"

"How do you know that they aren't?" said Bill, with a wry grin.

Mary smiled at his little joke as the door whooshed open, and they entered the room. The rest of her team, along with the people from Engineering, were already seated around the Plexiglas and aluminum conference table.

"Nice of you to join us," said Pinkus sarcastically as Billy and Mary took their seats. "As Project Manager, I would expect you would be here first."

"Sorry, Mr. Pinkus, it won't happen again," said Mary, kowtowing to the CEO. Pinkus nodded to her and then turned his attention to Zakari. "Okay, Professor, now that everyone is present, if you would?"

The professor rose from his chair and walked to the front of the conference table. "Believe it or not, there really is no law of physics preventing time travel," he said with no preamble. "Isaac Newton thought that time was like an arrow; once you fired it, it flew in a straight line, never deviating from its path, rendering time travel impossible. Then Einstein comes along and flipped the Newtonian view of things on end and declared that time is like a river, meandering its way around the universe."

The professor lightly touched a remote control in his hand, and a 3-D holographic image of the cosmos began whirling above the conference table.

"If we accept the idea of time as a river, then that River of Time can have eddies and whirlpools, and it can bend and fork." The image of the stars and nebulae was replaced with a gently flowing river.

Billy elbowed Jonny Roberts, who was seated next to him, and said, "Are we planning the next company Outward Bound river rafting trip or building a time machine?" Pinkus glared at him. The professor cleared his throat and continued. The river was again replaced with the image of the universe, which began spinning.

"If the universe rotated and you could travel around the outside of it," Zakari continued, "you could come back before you left."

Mary interjected, "But I thought Einstein said the universe is expanding, not rotating."

"Very good, Mary," the professor complimented her. "I see at least someone on this project has done her homework. You are quite correct; however, since Einstein said that the universe does not rotate, we have found many examples in which time travel would not conflict with Einstein's equations of an expanding universe. Wormholes, for example."

"Wormholes?" asked Jonny.

"Tear a piece of paper from your notepad there, if you would, Jonny, and hand it to me."

Jonny complied and slid the paper across the conference table to Zakari. "A wormhole works like this." He drew two dots on the piece of paper and folded it in half so the two dots met. "We can fold space and make two very distant points in space — or time — meet just like that. The only problem is that, according to Einstein's theories, such shortcuts in space-time require enormous amounts of energy, like that put out by an exploding, or collapsing, star. Energy far beyond anything we could harness or create on Earth."

"Until now, that is," Rick Roth from Engineering chimed in and rose from his seat. He took the remote control from the professor as they exchanged places. "Professor Zakari is absolutely right. We have known for a long time that wormholes exist, and for a long time we felt they would be the paths of least resistance when building a time machine. But a wormhole time machine presents many practical problems — not the least of which are the energy requirements the good doctor has mentioned. Are these insurmountable problems? Maybe not, but can they be solved within the delivery schedule required for this project? Definitely not — which got us thinking in another direction."

Rick clicked the remote. Again, the image of space appeared, only this time with an intense beam of light arcing through it.

"Light." Rick paused for effect. "Intense gravity like that created around a wormhole is not the only thing that can bend space-time; light can, as well."

Pinkus interrupted, "I'm no physicist, Rick, but I think I know where you are going. According to Einstein, time slows down as you approach the speed of light, but if you thought using wormholes for time travel was difficult, faster-than-light travel is even more impossible. I've had the boys in the Aerospace division working on that for years now, and they haven't even come close."

Rick smiled. "Ah, but we are not talking about moving faster than the speed of light. In fact, just the opposite – we have demonstrated that light can be slowed down – even brought to a virtual standstill." In the space above the conference table, a 3-D image of a spinning cylinder of light appeared, and within the tube, a snake-like twisted coil formed.

"If you take a series of mirrors spinning in a precise pattern reflecting slow-light at a specific point in space, we can create a vortex that should open a door in time."

Mary asked, somewhat confused, "Slow-light? I don't understand, Rick. That just doesn't make any sense."

"You don't have to understand it," Rick said, clicking off the Holo-projector. "Just give my team and I the green light, find our funding and we'll have you proof of concept in ten weeks."

Chapter 9: PM Foundations

Few weeks later, Mary called a team meeting in the main conference room. She stood in front of the room and addressed the group as a stranger stood beside her.

"As you know, this is a very ambitious project – probably our most ambitious ever, and Rick and his engineering group have certainly laid down the gauntlet with a ten-week timeline to prove our concept." The group nodded their acknowledgment.

Mary continued. "That is why I'd like to introduce you all to Peter Myste," she said, turning to the smartly dressed young man beside her. "He is going to introduce us to the techniques of PMBOK® Guide, which will help us all reach our goals."

"PMBOK® Guide?" said Billy. "What's that, some kind of Oriental card game?"

"No, not exactly, Mr. ahh. . ." Pete looked down at a digital clipboard in his hand. "Mr. Bragg." He walked over to a white board and wrote as he spoke. "PMBOK stands for 'The – Project – Management – Body – of Knowledge.'" He underlined the words.

"The PMBOK® Guide is a collection of best practice processes and knowledge for project management. No, Billy, it's not a game, but it will give you the strategies you need to win!" Pete continued to write on the white board. "Now, no matter what type of project you're working on, whether building a bridge, designing a new weapon system, or," he said, smiling, "building a time machine, the PMBOK® Guide recognizes five key steps in project management." Again, he wrote on the board.

Initiating

Planning

Executing

Monitoring and Controlling

Closing

"Now, Mary has actually brought me in a little late in the game. You all have already gone through steps 1 and 2, and we are now in step 3." Pete underlined 'Executing.' "But it's never too late to get on the right track with PMBOK® Guide tools." He turned his attention back to those gathered around the table.

"Now, if you will all open your smart-phones, you will see that the Project Management App has already been loaded. This will also automatically synch to your workstations or any other portable devices you will be using during the extent of this project."

Everyone opened their handhelds and accessed the App.

"I'll go over some of the basics, but you will find complete tutorials within each of the tools. As you scroll through, you will see things such as our Communications Management Plan, which defines the communications requirements for the project and how project information will be distributed and disseminated. I cannot stress enough how critical effective communication is to the success of this or any other project, and that is why the Communications Management Plan should be one of your key subsidiary plans."

Everyone began to navigate around the applications on their handsets. Pete continued, "The Project Management Plan provides the framework for managing the project. The Project Management Plan will take you through how the project is executed, monitored, controlled and finally closed."

Next, Pete directed his attention to Dottie Doodle, the CFO. "The Cost Management plan and Procurement Management Plan are two sub-plans that you would probably make more use of than the others, Dottie."

The team spent the remainder of the meeting with Pete, who drilled them in a crash-course on PMBOK® Guide methodology. Though they groused and complained initially, by the conclusion of the six-hour session, Pete was satisfied that his "cadets" had made it through Project Management "boot camp" and were on their way to a successful outcome.

Chapter 10: Project Execution

Mary began her day exactly as she had for the past few weeks, by logging on to her Scheduling Tool and immediately accessing *Project Document Updates*. She was surprised to find that the most recent in the queue was a report on the latest tests, as well as a memo from Rick Roth, stating that thanks to the diligence of the Management Team, he had scheduled a demonstration of the scale-model *Proof*

of Concept Time Machine next Wednesday. That was a full week and half ahead of schedule!

Mary smiled and said to herself, "I have to hand it to you, Mr. Myste, despite being a PMP, I must say, there really is something to this *PMBOK® Guide* stuff." Mary put the meeting into her Project Schedule and sent a personal note to Pete to thank him for all his help in whipping her team into shape.

On "demonstration day," Mary made sure she was the first to arrive at Roth's lab. Pinkus and the rest of the team soon joined her, including Pete Myste.

They all stood before a darkened, glass-enclosed chamber as Rick spoke to the group, his back to the window. "Now, as you know, by following the Communications Management Plan initiated by Mr. Myste," Rick said, nodding to Pete, "and by following your project documents and referring to our status updates, we were able to provide Proof of Concept. We devised an experiment to observe a **time-traveling neutron in a circulating beam of light.**"

Rick motioned to one of the technicians seated at a console near the group, and the lights in the chamber snapped on. On a pedestal in the center of the room sat something that looked like a toy carousel with mirrors. A technician dressed in a HAZMAT suit was standing by.

"Einstein's equations basically showed us that there really is very little difference between mass and energy. The time machine we've designed uses light in the form of circulating lasers to warp or loop time instead of using massive objects like wormholes. We know that certain subatomic particles, such as neutrinos, have a very short lifespan. At my signal, Karl in there will place a suspension rich in neutrinos in the center of those mirrors. By bombarding that with slow light lasers reflecting from the mirrors, if my theories are correct, we will see that those particles exist for a longer time than they normally would. A longer lifespan means that the particles would have flowed through a time loop and into the future. Under normal conditions, when not exposed to the slowed light, the particles would break down in a matter of seconds."

Rick flicked a switch on a panel on his side of the glass that activated a microphone. "Okay, Karl, if you would."

Karl went over to a small lead cube, opened it and removed a vial with long tongs. He turned and placed the vial in the center of the mirrors and backed out of the chamber. When Rick was sure he was clear, he touched a series of buttons on the console. The mirrors began to spin and whir, and a small column of light formed around the vial in its center. After a minute or so, they slowly wound down to a stop.

Pinkus said, "So?" Rick answered, "So now we watch." A technician seated behind the group spoke up. "Five seconds, still stable; 10 seconds, 15, 20 and still holding." Rick smiled broadly, "Ladies and gentlemen, welcome to the future."

SECTION 6

MONITORING AND CONTROLLING
THE PROJECT

Monitoring and controlling the project "in plain terms"

While the work is being executed according to the plan, the project manager and the team should be involved in monitoring and controlling the work being accomplished. It could consist of the project team members checking their work results and ensuring their results are accurate. At the same time it could consist of other endeavors in which the project manager and the team review work results of other individuals such as vendors, contractors or other resources external to the project. The project team also ensures that work progresses as documented in the project management plan. The monitoring and controlling efforts ensure that final deliverables are defect free.

This is a very important step in project management. The project manager and the team must decide on how best to monitor and control project work. This involves various processes such as controlling scope, schedule and costs. It also involves monitoring and controlling risks, managing contracts and administering procurements.

Controlling Changes

Another important part of the Monitoring and Controlling Process Group is to ensure that all change requests are processed correctly. All change requests should be formally documented and reviewed first by the Project Manager and then by a team known as the Change Control Board (CCB). This should be done through a process known as "Perform Integrated Change Control". This will ensure that all changes requested go through a formal review process and eventually may be either approved or rejected. If those change requests are approved then the changes will be fed back to the Executing Process Group processes to ensure all changes are executed on the project. Once executed, the changes will be reviewed again to verify all changes were accurately implemented.

Project Scope should be controlled; otherwise the project may go out of scope. You may find team members performing tasks as they like on the project and adding features that are not required. The schedule should also be controlled otherwise stakeholders may end up marching to their own beat, doing things when they want to as opposed to how the activities have been scheduled.

The Project Manager should also control costs because at the end of the day, if you do not control costs, you may have some team members spending resources or money however they can while trying to get you to sign off on it. This is not uncommon especially when some of the team may have the permission to sign off on certain purchases, charge to a credit card, or charge to a cost center. To prevent cost overruns and to curb unauthorized spending, ensure that you monitor and control all these different components.

35 Monitor and Control Project Work

This involves monitoring and controlling project activities and processes required to meet performance objectives defined in the Project Management Plan. The Monitor and Control Project Work process involves the following:

- Constant tracking, reviewing, monitoring and controlling project work.
- Collecting, measuring and distributing project performance information.
- Analyzing measurements and trends for effective process improvements.
- Monitoring project health throughout the project life.
- Comparing actual performance to planned performance.
- Assessing proposed corrective or preventive actions, recommending options and monitoring the implementation of approved changes.

Providing forecasts, identifying new risks, analysis, tracking, monitoring and executing of risk plans.

Inputs	Tools and Techniques	Outputs
Project management plan Schedule forecasts Cost forecasts Validated changes Work performance information Enterprise environmental factors Organization process assets	Expert judgment Analytical techniques Project management information system Meetings	Change requests Work performance reports Project management plan updates Project documents updates

Figure 40: Monitor and Control Project Work: Inputs, Tools & Techniques and Outputs

36 Perform Integrated Change Control

The Perform Integrated Change Control process involves controlling scope and project changes through the timely review of all change requests by approving or rejecting changes to deliverables, organizational process assets, project documents, Project Management Plan and other components. Integrated change control is achieved by influencing factors circumventing integrated change control and performing the following:

- Reviewing, analyzing, approving or denying change requests in a timely way.
- Maintaining baseline integrity: implementing only approved changes.
- Coordinating changes impacting schedule, cost, risk, quality and staffing.
- Documenting the impact of change requests.

All change requests must be approved or rejected by the Change Control Board (CCB) or some other relevant authority. All change requests should be documented and stored whether approved or rejected with explanations for approval or rejection. Although the Project Manager does not make the final decision, the Project Manager should be involved in receiving the formal change request from the customer and analyzing the request to determine how it impacts the triple constraint or other project aspects. The Project Manager should then submit the request and analysis to the CCB to make a final decision. The Project Manager may attend change control meetings or be a member of the CCB.

Inputs	Tools and Techniques	Outputs
◦ Project management plan ◦ Work performance reports ◦ Change requests ◦ Enterprise environmental factors ◦ Organizational process assets	◦ Expert judgment ◦ Meetings ◦ Change control tools	◦ Approved change requests ◦ Change log ◦ Project management plan updates ◦ Project documents updates

Figure 41: Perform Integrated Change Control

37   Validate Scope

Validate Scope is the process of obtaining formal customer or sponsor acceptance of the completed project deliverables. This should be sign-off of a formally issued document. In the event of premature project closure or termination, the Validate Scope process should establish the level and extent of completion.

Validate Scope is concerned with the customer's acceptance of the deliverable while Control Quality is concerned with the correctness of the deliverable and is performed by the seller. Both could be performed in parallel.

Inputs	Tools and Techniques	Outputs
<ul><li>Project management plan</li><li>Requirements documentation</li><li>Requirements traceability matrix</li><li>Verified deliverables</li><li>Work performance data</li></ul>	<ul><li>Inspection</li><li>Group decision-making techniques</li></ul>	<ul><li>Accepted deliverables</li><li>Change requests</li><li>Work performance information</li><li>Project documents updates</li></ul>

Figure 42: Validate Scope: Inputs, Tools & Techniques and Outputs

38 Control Scope

The Control Scope process involves controlling unnecessary ad-hoc unauthorized changes to the project scope of work. It also involves the following:

- Monitoring status of the project.

- Monitoring product scope.

- Managing changes to the scope baseline.

- Ensuring change requests, recommended preventive action and recommended corrective actions are performed through the Perform Integrated Change Control process.

- Preventing ad-hoc unauthorized random additions (known as gold plating) to project deliverables and objectives.

- Managing changes dynamically as they occur.

- Preventing scope creep (uncontrolled changes) to the Scope Baseline.

The Scope Baseline should be monitored, verified and controlled throughout the project's life-cycle.

Inputs	Tools and Techniques	Outputs
<ul><li>Project management plan</li><li>Requirements documentation</li><li>Requirements traceability matrix</li><li>Work performance data</li><li>Organizational process assets</li></ul>	<ul><li>Variance analysis</li></ul>	<ul><li>Work performance information</li><li>Change requests</li><li>Project management plan updates</li><li>Project document updates</li><li>Organizational process assets updates</li></ul>

Figure 43: Control Scope: Inputs, Tools & Techniques and Outputs

39 Control Schedule

In this process the Project Manager is involved in monitoring schedule status to update project progress and determining if a schedule change has occurred or may need to occur. Some of the responsibilities of the Project Manager here involve:

- Managing changes to the schedule baseline.
- Influencing factors which contribute to schedule change.
- Managing & controlling changes to the schedule promptly.

Before changes are made to a schedule, the impact of these changes should be assessed and discussed with all relevant parties. Any change requests on the project should become an input to the Perform Integrated Change Control process.

Inputs	Tools and Techniques	Outputs
<ul><li>Project Management Plan</li><li>Project Schedule</li><li>Work performance data</li><li>Project calendar</li><li>Schedule data</li><li>Organizational process assets</li></ul>	<ul><li>Performance reviews</li><li>Project management software</li><li>Resource optimization techniques</li><li>Modeling techniques</li><li>Leads and lags</li><li>Schedule Compression</li><li>Scheduling Tool</li></ul>	<ul><li>Work performance information</li><li>Schedule forecasts</li><li>Change requests</li><li>Project management plan updates</li><li>Project documents updates</li><li>Organizational process assets Updates</li></ul>

Figure 44: Control Schedule: Inputs, Tools & Techniques and Outputs

40 Control Cost

Control Costs involves monitoring and controlling expenditure of funds on a project to update the project budget. The following are also part of this process:

- Managing changes to the cost baseline.
- Recording actual costs spent to date.
- Approving cost changes through the approved integrated change control process.
- Influencing factors that cause changes to the cost baseline.
- Acting on change requests immediately.
- Ensuring actual cost does not exceed planned cost.
- Monitoring costs to understand variances from the approved cost baseline.
- Reasons for variances being understood and preventive action taken.

Monitoring work performance against funds expected.

Inputs	Tools and Techniques	Outputs
Cost management plan Human resource plan Scope baseline Project schedule Risk register Enterprise environmental factors Organizational process assets	Expert judgment Analogous estimating Parametric estimating Bottom-up estimating Three-Point estimates Reserve analysis Cost of quality Project management software Vendor bid analysis Group decision-making techniques	Activity cost estimates Basis of estimates Project documents updates

Figure 45: Estimate Costs: Inputs, Tools & Techniques and Outputs

41 Control Quality

The Control Quality process involves minimizing and controlling variation through preferably prevention and inspection. The Project Manager is responsible for monitoring and documenting specific project results to verify if they comply with the relevant quality standards and identifying ways to eliminate causes of unsatisfactory performance by identifying and controlling deviation from quality. Quality control is achieved through:

- Prevention: keeping errors out of the process.
- Inspection: keeping errors out of the customer's reach.

Quality processes interact with processes in other Knowledge Areas as well. Quality management may involve a coordinated effort across several groups. Project Quality Management applies to both management of the project and the product of the project.

Inputs	Tools and Techniques	Outputs
Project management Plan Quality metrics Quality checklists Work performance data Approved change requests Deliverables Project documents Organizational process assets	Seven basic quality tools Statistical sampling Inspection Approved change request review	Quality control measurements Validated changes Verified deliverables Work performance information Change requests Project management plan updates Project document updates Organizational process assets updates

Figure 46: Control Quality: Inputs, Tools & Techniques and Outputs

42   Control Communications

Control Communications involves monitoring and controlling communications to ensure stakeholder communication needs are being met. In the process, the project manager should ensure the stakeholders receive all manner of expected communications at the right time. The project manager should also be proactive to ensure delivered communications meet stakeholder needs.

Inputs	Tools and Techniques	Outputs
• Project management Plan • Project communications • Issue log • Work performance data • Organizational process assets	• Information management systems • Expert judgment • Meetings	• Work performance information • Change request • Project management plan updates • Project documents updates • Organizational process assets updates

Figure 47: Control Communications: Inputs, Tools & Techniques and Outputs

43 Control Risk

The Control Risks process involves implementing risk response plans for identifying, analyzing and tracking risks (both old and new). The activities carried out during this process may include:

- Tracking identified risks and those on a watch list.
- Re-analyze existing risks.
- Monitoring risk conditions.
- Also applied are techniques such as variance and trend analysis.

The Control Risks process should occur throughout the project to determine:

- If project assumptions are still valid.
- If a risk has changed from its prior state.
- Adherence to risk management policies and procedures.
- Modification of contingency reserves if risks in the project change.

Inputs	Tools and Techniques	Outputs
● Project management plan ● Risk register ● Work performance data ● Work performance reports	● Risk reassessment ● Risk audits ● Variance and trend analysis ● Technical performance measurement ● Reserve analysis ● Meetings	● Work performance information ● Change requests ● Project management plan updates ● Project document updates ● Organizational process assets updates

Figure 48: Control Risks: Inputs, Tools & Techniques and Outputs

44 Control Procurements

The Control Procurements process entails reviewing and documenting how well the team is performing; ensuring that both parties meet their contractual obligations. Certain organizations may treat this process separately though a legal department or with strong legal counsel involvement. It is important that the project management team is familiar with legal implications of contracts and any actions taken when administering procurements. On large projects, a key aspect of administering procurements is managing interfaces among the various vendors or service providers

Control Procurements involves:

- Establishing corrective action if the seller's work is not progressing as planned.
- Ensuring that both party's legal rights are protected.
- Applying the right project management processes to contractual relationships.
- Monitoring payments to the seller and ensuring that they are paid as agreed in the contract.
- Managing early terminations of contracts (for specific causes, convenience or default).
- Modifying contracts prior to contract closure with mutual consent from both parties.

Inputs	Tools and Techniques	Outputs
Project management Plan Procurement documents Agreements Approved change requests Work performance reports Work performance data	Contract change control system Procurement performance reviews Inspections and audits Performance reporting Payment systems Claims administration Records management system	Work performance information Change requests Project management plan updates Project documents updates Organizational process assets updates

Figure 49: Control Procurements: Inputs, Tools & Techniques and Outputs

45 Control Stakeholder Engagement

In this process, the Project Manager is involved in monitoring and controlling stakeholder relationships. If stakeholder relationships are unfavorable, re-planning of stakeholder management strategies or execution of these strategies may be necessary to effectively engage stakeholders.

Effectively controlling stakeholder engagement will maintain or increase the efficiency and effectiveness of stakeholder engagement activities as the project evolves.

Inputs	Tools and Techniques	Outputs
<ul><li>Project Management Plan</li><li>Issue Log</li><li>Work Performance Data</li><li>Project Documents</li></ul>	<ul><li>Information Management Systems</li><li>Expert Judgment</li><li>Meetings</li></ul>	<ul><li>Work Performance Information</li><li>Change Requests</li><li>Project management Plan Updates</li><li>Project Documents Updates</li><li>Organizational Process Assets Updates</li></ul>

Figure 50: Control Stakeholder Engagement: Inputs, Tools & Techniques and Outputs

Monitoring and Controlling Process Group Summary

In the Monitoring and Controlling Process Group, as the word monitoring implies, this is where the Project Manager and the team monitor and control the project. Activities are monitored to ensure work is progressing as planned. If the Project Manager discovers that the project is not progressing as planned, then the situation must be controlled. The Project Manager monitors the project and controls the project work based on project progress and reports. The processes in the Monitoring and Controlling Process Group are critical for delivery of an accurate and precise deliverable that conforms to all the stakeholder's requirements. The processes in this Process Group span across every aspect of the project in the project life-cycle up to the point where all sub-deliverables from vendors are confirmed complete and final deliverables are accepted by the customer in formal writing.

Group Discussion
1. Briefly discuss what it means to monitor and control the project and activities you would expect to occur in this Process Group.
2. Discuss activities you would expect to occur before and after the Perform Integrated Change Control Process.

Monitoring and Controlling Process Group Real-World Project Work

a. **Project Performance Report**
   Due to potential problems with system customizations implemented for your client, your senior management *(including the project sponsor, project portfolio management group, Project Management Office or other project oversight person or group in your organization)* has asked for a weekly report on your project. Complete a Project Performance Report to satisfy this requirement.

b. **Variance Analysis**
   Due to the recent system customizations implemented for your client, there have been changes in the project since your last project performance report to senior management. You want to highlight significant changes in schedule, cost, and quality resulting from customizations on the project. Complete a Variance Analysis to better capture and assemble all the information on these performance variances and send that together with the Project Performance report to senior management.

c. **Earned Value Analysis**
   Your client is required by the government to report specific metrics designed to reflect the health of their projects by integrating scope, schedule, and cost

information. To meet this requirement, list out for your team a suggestion of metrics to include in this Earned Value Analysis report.

Product Acceptance

The major deliverable from your product has been accepted. To document acceptance by your client, complete a Product Acceptance form to record all new and old requirements, method of verification and validation.

Chapter 11: Making Progress

The anticipation was palpable as the Project Team gathered outside Roth's lab for the first test of the full-scale prototype Time Machine, which he had coined TMX.01. It had taken years to prototype! Each member of the team donned white "bunny suits" in the outer chamber before entering the clean room.

"Come in, come in," said Roth excitedly. He held a small chimpanzee, which clung to him very closely. Behind him was a full-sized prototype of the scale-model mirror arrays that had been tested successfully those many months ago.

"This is Wells," he said, nodding toward the primate.

"Wells, as in H.G.?" said Mary, smiling, "Very cute, Rick."

Liz, who was there to take notes, looked at her, dumbfounded. Jonny snorted and said, "Oh, come on, Liz, H.G. Wells? — The Time Machine? You know — the book?"

Liz just continued to look oblivious.

Rick shook his head and said, "Be that as it may, Wells here is going to be our first little time traveler. I plan to test the TMX.01 by sending him two days hence."

Pinkus asked, "But how will you know if it worked?"

"Good question, and if you will all look at your work flows, you will see that I have a meeting scheduled right here at this exact time two days from now. Wells should show up in the TMX machine and find us waiting here for him."

"Mind-boggling," said Jonny.

"Indeed," agreed Roth. "Well, let's get started, shall we?"

Wells looked a bit frightened as Roth placed him into a cage in the center of the mirrors, as Karl had done with the vial of isotopes during the Proof of Concept test. "Everyone, step back behind the safety glass, please," Roth instructed.

He continued. "Initiating time sequence in 5-4-3-2-1"

On "one," the mirrors began to spin, and the chamber filled with a rising hum. A column of golden light shot up from the center of the mirrors where the chimp was secured. From within the column of light, the chimp let out a blood-curdling scream.

Rick shouted, "Shut it down! Shut it down!" The mirrors wound to a stop, the column of light disappeared and Wells slumped to the floor of his cage, twitching in agony.

Roth ran to the stricken chimp's side. Liz started to cry and buried her head in Jonny's chest.

Mary said, "What is it, Rick, what happened?"

Rick looked down at the quivering chimp. Its fur was patchy and thin and completely gray where it remained; its eyes were cloudy and shot. Wells soon stopped shaking and rolled over, its vacant eyes staring at the ceiling.

"I'm not certain," Roth replied, concerned. "I will have to run some tests to be sure, but if I could guess, I'd say instead of moving into the future, Wells just died of extreme old age."

Pinkus looked down in disgust at the chimp's still form. "Clean up that mess, Roth. I was against this project from the get-go. You have ten days to figure out what went wrong and give me a working prototype, or the Board is going to make monkeys out of all of us!"

"If you fell down yesterday, stand up today."
H. G. Wells

SECTION 8

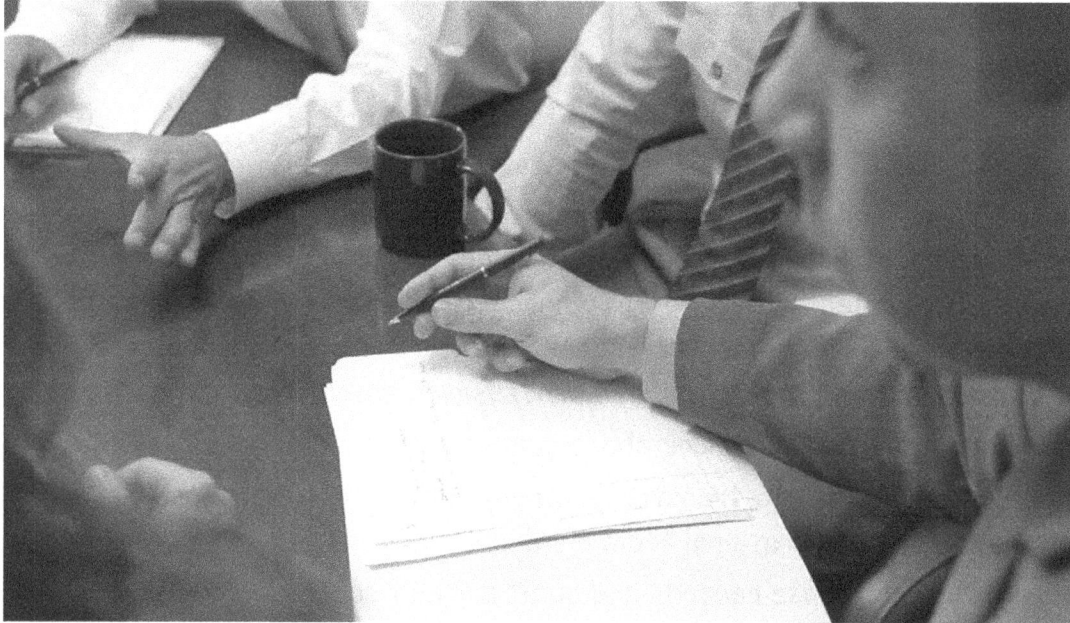

CLOSING THE PROJECT

The final stage in project management is the closing stage. In closing out a project, the project team has several tasks to carry out. The most important tasks are to verify that all the work has been captured in the deliverable or the requirements are inherent in the deliverable. Before the closing process group, the project manager should have already ensured that the deliverable meets all the requirements of the stakeholders and the customers should have already given formal approval in writing.

In the closing process group the deliverable is transitioned to the customer. In the real world, formal acceptance and final product service or result transition (which is an output of the Close Project or Phase process) could actually happen in quick succession. It could happen within a space of a few minutes, hours or days, but the most important thing is that you understand what exactly is happening and when. It is also important to understand there is a difference between transitioning a product, service or result to the customer and getting approval on a product, service or result. These are both different steps recognized in the PMBOK Guide Fourth Edition.

46   Close Project or Phase

The Close Project or Phase process involves finalizing all activities across all Project Management Process Groups to formally close a project or phase. When closing out the project, the Project Manager should review information from previous phase closures and ensure that all the work has been completed and that the project has met all objectives. This process also establishes:

- Actions and activities to ensure phase completion or exit criteria.
- Actions and activities to transfer the project to the next phase or transition the project to the operational team.
- Actions to collect phase records and audit project success.
- Procedures for managing premature project termination (for early project termination to take place, both parties should be in agreement).

Procedures for lessons learned collection and archiving.

Inputs	Tools and Techniques	Outputs
Project management plan Accepted deliverables Organizational process assets	Expert judgment Analytical techniques Meetings	Final product, service or result transition Organizational process assets updates

Figure 51: Close Project or Phase: Inputs, Tools & Techniques and Outputs

Lesson Learned

Project Title:	TMX 01

Project Sponsor:	Alfred Pinkus and Jonny Roberts	Date Prepared:	12-Aug-49
Project Manager:	Mary Johnson	Project Customer:	Professor Zakari

Purpose

This document is intended to gather or summarize the lessons learned in the execution of the project in order to facilitate the project managers who are in similar track. This aims to document the problems that occurred and how they were handled so they can be avoided in the future. Moreover, it will detail what went well and why, who the team members were for planning their projects in the future. This document will be formally communicated and will become a part of organizational process assets.

Lesson Learned

Category	Problem/Success	Impact	Recommendation
Scope Management	The sponsor wanted the GS64-M research to be included during the cosmic research in order to help solve the limitation of blue holes.	More than USD 10 million was required to integrate this during cosmic research	From next project this practice should be followed. This will help avoid scope creep.
Quality Management	A process for standard quality policies was planned.	Allowed team to work to ensure all materials were of acceptable quality and avoided any rework and delays.	From next project this practice should be followed. This helps avoid delays and cost overruns.
Risk Management	Risk identification was planned to be performed throughout the project execution but was not employed during the middle of the project.	More than USD150000 was spent due to Galactus Robote sparking loss during Gravitation research	From next project a practice should be introduced to allocate minimum number of risk review at any specific duration.
Procurement Management	Previous lesson learned recommendation about contractor handling was not followed that caused delivery of low quality Aqua Hunger Force Controller device	Customer was unsatisfied with the device. Also, it delayed the project for 3 months	From next project, previous recommendation should be taken into account.
Time Management	Activity time estimates were done by three point estimate that ensure validated time frame most of the cases.	Allowed team to provide required time to work each and every activity	This practice should be followed across the organization go forward.
Cost Management	Some activity cost estimates were done by parametric estimate that did not match with practical situation.	Some activity cost increments	From next project, other estimating practices like three point estimates should be taken into account.

Form 31: Lessons Learned

47   Close Procurements

Several projects require various inputs from several vendors to produce a final deliverable. Close Procurements is the process of completing & closing out procurements with each vendor. Close Procurements supports the Close Project or Phase process and involves final confirmation that all work and deliverables from the vendors is acceptable.

Activities in this process are aimed at closing out each contract/procurement applicable to the project or phase. The Project Manager should also be aware that:

- Finalizing open claims and updating records is important.
- Unresolved claims may be subject to litigation.
- Contract terms and conditions should prescribe procedures for contract closure.
- Early termination of a contract is also considered as procurement closure under the following conditions:
    - When both parties are in agreement
    - If a party defaults
    - For convenience of the buyer (if provided for in the contract).

Buyer may have to compensate seller for any completed work or deliverables.

Inputs	Tools and Techniques	Outputs
Project management plan Procurement documentation	Procurement audits Negotiated settlements Records management system	Closed procurements Organizational process assets updates

Figure 52: Close Procurements: Inputs, Tools & Techniques and Outputs

Closing Process Group Summary

The order of closing a project should be as follows:
- Transition of the deliverable to the customer
- Lessons learned and other pertinent closing documentation completed, reviewed and archived by the team
- Release of project resources.

Group Discussion
a) Discuss what must happen before a project is closed.
b) Discuss the key activities the team is involved in when closing a project.

Closing Process Group Real-World Project Work

a. Complete a Contract Close-out to document and evaluate the performance of vendor(s).

b. Complete a Project Close-out to document the final project performance in cost, schedule, quality, risk and resources. You will do this by reviewing project objectives and documenting your evidence of meeting those objectives.

c. Complete a Lessons Learned document and identify 2 things that went well on the project, 2 things that need to be improved and suggestions for improvement.

Chapter 12: A Second Try

A few months after the horrible, failed experiment with Wells, the team again gathered in Roth's lab. Memories of what had transpired the last time still haunted Mary and sent chills down her spine.

A 3-D CAD image of the TMX and its schematics rotated in the air before them. "I don't know, gang, I have been over it and over it," Rick began. "I know what happened to Wells, but I still can't understand why it happened. Everything should have worked perfectly, as it did with the small-scale proof-of-concept."

"Rick, may I?" said Pete, stepping forward unexpectedly.

"You?" Rick gave Pete an incredulous look, and then sighed. "Sure, why not, I'm done." Rick said with exasperation.

"Don't give up, Rick, you are so close. Not only have you used proper Project Management to get us this far," Pete nodded to the rest of the team, acknowledging that they had done the same, "but your theories, your concept, even your engineering protocols are all sound —it's your algorithms that are a little off."

Pete replaced the holo display of the TMX with a complex series of mathematical equations. "You see, Rick," Pete said, as he started manipulating the figures with his fingertips, "You just have to change the value of photovoltaics here, then adjust the gravimetric pulse cycles like this, so that the EMP and IR sine waves now look like this."

"My gosh, he's right!" exclaimed Rick. The equation flashed green.

"Try it now," said Pete, smiling broadly.

Rick once again engaged the mirrors. The lab began to hum, and a golden cylinder of shimmering light formed from floor to ceiling. As the cylinder glowed more intensely, the Project Team stared in awe as a vortex, an actual ripple in time, slowly appeared within.

Rick cried out in astonishment, shouting over the whine of the spinning mirror array. "But, Pete, how could you possibly know the right equation? You're no engineer, and we have been working on that theorem unsuccessfully for days now."

Pete just smiled, and before anyone could say a word or raise an objection, he stepped inside the glowing vortex! As his body began to discorporate in a swirling cosmic glow, he said, "See you in about twenty years, and I'll let you know!" And he was gone — swallowed by the time stream. The mirrors slowly ground to a halt, and the pillar of light disappeared.

For a moment, no one spoke, and then Pinkus broke the stunned silence. "Can someone please explain to me what just happened here?"

Mary smiled. "Remember when Pete first joined this team, how out of place he seemed, like he wasn't from around here?" The team nodded. "Well, that's because he wasn't!" she said, smiling.

Rick completed her thought in sudden realization, "We *did* build the Time Machine, and we made it work, but only because Pete used it to come back from the future and give me the very formula I needed to do so!"

- The End -